Designing the Digital Experience

How to Use Experience Design Tools and Techniques to Build Websites Customers Love

David Lee King

CyberAge Books

Information Today, Inc.
Medford, New Jersey

First printing, 2008

Designing the Digital Experience: How to Use Experience Design Tools and Techniques to Build Websites Customers Love

Library of Congress Cataloging-in-Publication Data

King, David Lee, 1966-
Designing the digital experience : how to use experience design tools and techniques to build Websites customers love / David Lee King.
p. cm.
Includes index.
ISBN 978-0-910965-83-5
1. Web sites--Design. I. Title.
TK5105.888.K5546 2008
006.7--dc22

2008034152

President and CEO: Thomas H. Hogan, Sr.
Editor-in-Chief and Publisher: John B. Bryans
Managing Editor: Amy M. Reeve
Project Editor: Rachel Singer Gordon
VP Graphics and Production: M. Heide Dengler
Book Designer: Kara Mia Jalkowski
Cover Designer: Lisa Boccadutre
Copyeditor: Bonnie Freeman
Proofreader: Barbara Brynko
Indexer: Sharon Hughes

www.infotoday.com

CONTENTS

PART 1: STRUCTURAL FOCUS

PART 2: COMMUNITY FOCUS

PART 3: CUSTOMER FOCUS

ACKNOWLEDGMENTS

In no particular order, I'd like to thank a bunch of people who, in one form or another, helped me write this book: Dana, my beautiful and highly intelligent wife, who made my words sound so much better; Kaitlyn, Nathan, and Lillabeth, who put up with Daddy's writing; God, who gave me the words in the first place; Rachel Singer Gordon, who encouraged me to write a book; Michael Stephens, Jenny Levine, and Steven M. Cohen—you don't know it, but y'all encouraged me to blog in the first place (so it's your fault!); David Armano, Jesse James Garrett, Kathy Sierra, and Jenny Levine, for the graphics; 37signals, for the extensive quotations; my blog/Twitter/Facebook/MySpace friends; and my blog readers, for much encouragement.

ABOUT THE WEB PAGE

www.davidleeking.com/digitalexperience

Information on *Designing the Digital Experience* will be found in two places on the author's blog at www.davidleeking.com. General information about the book can be found at www.davidleeking.com/digitalexperience; updated content related to the book can be found at www.davidleeking.com/category/digitalexperience. Readers will find live links to sites mentioned in the book and to other related content.

Disclaimer

Neither the publisher nor the author makes any claim as to the results that may be obtained through the use of this web page or of any of the Internet resources it references or links to. Neither publisher nor author will be held liable for any results, or lack thereof, obtained by the use of this page or any of its links; for any third-party changes; or for any hardware, software, or other problems that may occur as the result of using it. This web page is subject to change or discontinuation without notice at the discretion of the publisher and author.

FOREWORD

Whether it be physical or digital, experience is everything. Think about it. We are living in an unprecedented time of change, uncertainty, and rapid advances in both technology and even human behavior. We've seen once thriving companies such as Tower Records close their doors because change happened so rapidly. We're witnessing niche players like Trader Joe's and Whole Foods nibble at the revenue once dominated by the mega supermarket chains. We've seen companies like Dell master the science of supply chain economics only to find themselves grappling with the competitive advantage they need to move further away from a commodity market. And while authors of business books would have you believe that social media is *the* story of the century, the real story is people and the relationships we have with not only each other but with the businesses and brands of the world that we choose to interact with throughout our lives. While a business like Dell has become a case study for successfully tapping the power of social networks, it still has to come to terms with itself at a "soul level": What's the quality of the collective experience that consumers have with it? And do those experiences lead to a sustainable affinity for the brand?

So if you went out and bought this book, you're heading in the right direction. The reason social networks are such a big deal these days is that they act as both the great equalizer and amplifier. Customers who have a bad experience with a company's products or services now have a virtual arsenal of communication methods to make their voices be heard. Often, Google's powerful algorithms find such content and links to complaints. When a certain "power consumer" couldn't cancel his AOL account despite several pleas with the voice on the other end of the phone, he decided to take matters into his own hands and record the horrendous experience. What resulted was a PR nightmare for AOL that started online, gained momentum, and was quickly reported on several national news stations. What starts digital becomes something much bigger, and it all starts with an experience.

Yes, the social revolution needs to be understood, but what needs to be driven home even more is that companies that continue to deliver mediocre or bad experiences will find themselves in a downward spiral, fueled by a digital revolution that has now empowered all of us. On the other hand, companies that figure out new ways to delight customers will have brighter futures and consumers who are more than happy to do their marketing for them. It sounds simple and seems like common sense because it is—but the reality is that few companies have customer service baked into their DNA and culture. The ones that don't may choose to go about business as usual, but will have to risk dealing with a better educated and empowered consumer class who are being influenced by the most influential source out there: *people just like them.*

As you read the pages of David Lee King's book and ponder the case studies, ask yourself these questions: Is your product or service worth talking about? Is there something about it that offers indisputable value even if your product is primarily web-based? Is it a meaningful experience? I often tell the story of when my wife and I wanted to sell one of our children's playsets. I woke up one Saturday morning and found my wife taking pictures of it. When I asked her what she was doing, she said, "I need you to take this apart so we can sell it." Without asking questions, I began to quickly disassemble the set. As I was doing this, my wife was busy uploading multiple photos on craigslist, the free online classified service. A while later as I was nearly finished with my work, she came over to me and said, "I think we have a buyer."

Sure enough, we did. In fact, in the few hours since she had listed the playset, we had several people who wanted to buy it and were willing to drive to our house and pick it up. By late afternoon, the most qualified buyer came and handed us $200 in cash, picked up the set, and drove off. We celebrated with a nice bottle of wine on the patio. Let me tell you that our experience with craigslist was useful, meaningful, and indeed delightful—despite the site's bare bones design. And, it's possibly a business killer. As I write this, the once mighty *Chicago Tribune* (which I worked for when first coming to Chicago) is struggling as its business model slowly is eroded by many factors, one of them being free digital classified services like craigslist that seemingly come out of nowhere.

So how do people find out about services like craigslist? Well, by hearing stories like the one I just told you. This is a story rooted in continuous positive interactions and ultimately a great experience that we have with the service. These experiences lead to affinity, loyalty, and ultimately a relationship with the brand. And, we're all too happy to trade the *Chicago Tribune* for craigslist—sorry, it's not personal. As you begin to dive into this book, think about all the signs of change around you. Then think about the things that do not change. We're all social beings, we all have to get our basic needs met, and we seek positive experiences while trying to avoid negative ones. Whether it be a website, product, or service, these are basic human truths. And it's why the strategy, planning, and execution of experiences are more important than they've possibly ever been.

David Armano

David Armano is both an active practitioner and thought leader in the worlds of experience design and digital marketing. Author of the popular Logic + Emotion blog, he currently works for Critical Mass, a digital agency focused on the creation of extraordinary experiences. He writes industry perspectives for *Ad Age* and *BusinessWeek* and is best known for his distinct brand of visual thinking, which can be found both on the web and in presentations all over the world.

INTRODUCTION

Visitors to an organization's digital space don't want to think about interacting with its website. They want to—quickly and easily—make a purchase, find information, or do research. It helps if they can be engaged and enchanted in the process. How can we facilitate this excellent experience? It's all about intentional design.

Consider the concept of "experience design." Nathan Shedroff describes it as designing the "sensation of interaction with a product, service, or event, through all of our senses, over time, and on both physical and cognitive levels."[1] Simply stated, experience design is "an approach to creating successful experiences for people in any medium."[2]

Designing *digital* experience is similar, yet unique. That's because in a digital space, experience designers have to "compensate for the absence of a sales professional who stands ready to greet customers as they arrive [and] to cheerfully help them accomplish their goal."[3]

This book introduces digital experience design for websites. I have seen great information on parts and pieces of experience design. For example, B. Joseph Pine II and James H. Gilmore's book, *The Experience Economy: Work Is Theatre & Every Business a Stage,* does a great job of exploring experience generally but really doesn't focus on digital experiences. Other books are great at helping improve the user experience on websites but miss the broader picture of designing digital experiences. This book connects the dots. It explains how website structure, community, and customers are all parts of the total digital experience.

Here's what you get: Chapter 1 defines what I mean by digital experience design. Then it discusses three aspects of designing digital experiences: what I call the structural, community, and customer focus.

Part 1 tackles the structural focus in digital experience design: creating better experiences by improving a website's ease of use. Great customer experiences happen when customers can focus on their own goals rather than on how to navigate your site. In Chapter 2, I explain what structural focus is. Chapter 3 compares three quite different models of experience design—Jesse James Garrett's *Elements of User Experience* model, David Armano's *Experience Map* model, and 37signals' *Getting Real* model of designing digital experiences. Chapter 4 explains information architecture and usability. It shows you how the experience design aspects of these concepts help provide a great user experience.

Part 2 explores the community focus in digital experience design. Memorable experiences are created via online participation and community. Chapters include an explanation of community focus in digital experience design (Chapter 5); how emerging digital tools such as blogs, wikis, podcasting, and videocasting can be used to create digital experiences (Chapter 6); and ways to actively build and invite conversations and community online (Chapter 7). Chapter 8 discusses how community and experience are created through social networking sites such as Flickr, YouTube, MySpace, Facebook, and Twitter, and how you can begin using these sites.

Finally, Part 3 addresses the customer focus. You will find out how to stage experiences online and get practical tips on how to turn negative and neutral experiences into positive and memorable ones. Chapter 9 introduces customer-focused digital experience design. Chapter 10 provides examples and best practices of staged digital experiences. Personas and customer journey mapping—great ways to focus a customer experience—are the topics of Chapter 11. Chapter 12 provides ideas to get you started creating customer-focused digital experience design, including improving the ordinary, updating dinosaurs, and using merit badging techniques.

Finally, Chapter 13 synthesizes the preceding chapters into examples of how a website might look if it included all three types of focus.

So, bring what you have to the table. Let's examine some blueprints and choose some tools so you can get busy and build the amazing digital experiences of the future. Your customers will be glad you did.

Endnotes

1. Nathan Shedroff, Nathan: Experience Design, nathan.com/ed (accessed January 28, 2008).

2. Shedroff.

3. Kevin Mullet, The Essence of Effective Rich Internet Applications (macromedia white paper), November 2003, download.macromedia.com/pub/solutions/downloads/business/essence_of_ria.pdf (accessed January 28, 2008).

CHAPTER 1

Welcome to the Experience Economy

What's my daughter playing on the computer this evening? Oh, she's on the American Girl site, and she's playing Kaya's Catch of the Day. She also sent an American Girl ecard to her cousin and looked at this year's new doll. We receive American Girl catalogs and magazines in the mail and check out the latest books from the library. We even visited American Girl Place in Chicago last winter as a birthday surprise (the girls and mom watched a musical, had a tea party, and shopped, while my son and I checked out the science museum and LEGO Store).

What's going on here? Why is my daughter so into this stuff? Because American Girl is all about the experience. It focuses on the fun of exploring and living as a girl in America's past. The American Girl people are engaging their market in creative ways—specifically targeting grade school and middle school girls. They know how to delight their customers. I know—I've seen my daughter's smiles. As we continue to think about experience, let's consider the experiences of a trip to an amusement park and the purchase of a computer.

Silver Dollar City

Have you visited Silver Dollar City, a popular theme park located in Branson, Missouri? My family visits the park a couple of times every year (my parents retired in Branson, so we have an added incentive). According to its website, "Silver Dollar City ... is one of the most popular vacation destinations in the country. Travel back in time to the simplicity of 1880s America."[1] The site elaborates even further on another page:

> Silver Dollar City ... combines the wholesome family fun of a major theme park with the timeless appeal of crafts and a dedication to preserving 1880s Ozarks culture. Over 100 craftsmen are on park demonstrating glass blowing, basket weaving, blacksmithing, pottery, candy making, candle making, and many other disciplines. Packed with over 20 rides and attractions, 60 unique shops and restaurants, and 40 dazzling shows a day, Silver Dollar City truly appeals to all ages. It also hosts five major festivals per year and was named one of the Top Theme Parks in the World by the International Association of Amusement Parks and Attractions.[2]

Why do we go back to the park year after year? For the "experience," of course.

Besides the fun theme rides, we love the old-timey stuff! It's quite fun to watch glassblowers and ride behind a steam-powered locomotive. The shows tend to be geared toward the park's theme as well, so lots of dulcimer and fiddle music can be heard. And, of course, everyone who works there is dressed as a character from the 1880s, and some of the rides even include brief historical snippets of the Ozarks in the 1880s.

We enjoy Silver Dollar City because it provides the complete package. We aren't going to the park just to ride a roller coaster or eat kettle corn. We're paying to participate in a version of 1880s southern Missouri and to have some memorable family-oriented fun in the process. We are there for the *experience.*

Buying an Apple

Let's move to a completely different type of experience: buying a laptop. But not just any laptop—an Apple. I bought my first laptop last summer. (I actually purchased it to write this book.) I bought the computer online at the Apple Store. It was a breeze. Apple's site is extremely easy to use. To get to the store, I simply clicked on "Store" from the main page. Each laptop is actually displayed on the main Store page! Fantastic! Ever bought a PC? Many PC makers have a lot of different laptop models, all hidden under a variety of model names and labels. Apple makes this part easy by having just two to choose from: the MacBook and the MacBook Pro (I went with the MacBook Pro).

Next, I had to pick the screen size (easy again) and had the option to upgrade the laptop a bit (which I did). The paying part was very familiar—similar to that of other large sites, such as Amazon.com. Again, easy as pie! This was a pleasing *experience.* Not once did I have to think about Apple's website, obtuse language, which oddly named laptop model I wanted, or how to work the page. Instead, I was able to think about what I wanted to do (choose and buy a laptop from Apple) the whole time.

I don't mean to evangelize for the Mac (although it's hard not to sound that way, because Apple gets many things right). But get this: I announced my purchase on my Flickr account, and I heard from other "evangelists"! Here's what some of my Flickr pals told me when I announced that I had just purchased a Mac:[3]

- "Nice work. What are you going to do with all that free time you spent cursing?"

- "One of us, one of us! Let's all chip in for David's tattoo— neck or wrist or elsewhere?" (The words *neck, wrist,* and *elsewhere* all pointed to pictures of actual tattoos people had gotten of the Apple logo!)

- "Rock on, David! life will never be the same :)"

It's not hard to see what went on here. Apple made the purchasing process extremely easy. It provided only enough choices to make me feel as if I had a choice (desktop vs. laptop, two laptop models), and it made the checkout process easy. And, of course, Apple computers simply work. I've had no problems so far. Apple is providing a great computer, but it's also providing a great computer *experience* that few, if any, of its competitors match.

What Is Experience?

You have now read about a few extremely different examples of experience. What exactly is experience, and how does it relate in any way, shape, or form to the web? Let's start that discussion off by introducing you to the experience economy.

If you want a thorough introduction to the experience economy, you should read *The Experience Economy: Work Is Theatre & Every Business a Stage,* by B. Joseph Pine II and James H. Gilmore. In a nutshell, Pine says, "It's crucial to understand that experiences are a distinct economic offering, as distinct from services as services are from goods. Experiences result when a company uses tangible

My "i just bought a mac" Flickr page with comments showing

goods as props and intangible services as the stage for engaging each customer in an inherently personal way."[4]

Pine and Gilmore's claim is that our economy is changing. People have enough money to buy whatever they want, and they don't simply want goods anymore; they can get goods anywhere. They can get service everywhere, but they don't want simply good service anymore, either. Instead, they want to go one further and buy an experience. Think about a restaurant, for example. You can go to McDonald's and buy a sandwich. Or you can go to Applebee's and buy a better, larger, tastier sandwich with better service. Or you can go to the Hard Rock Cafe, have a rock star experience, and get a meal along with it. That's buying an experience.

These experiences are often purposely designed or staged. "The experience is the marketing. The best way to market any product is with an experience so engaging that potential customers can't help but pay attention—and pay up as a result by buying that product."[5] The goal is to stage an experience for the customer that is so engaging that people can't help but purchase it!

Digital Experience

But wait, isn't this book about designing *digital* experiences? Where's the connection? You can also stage and design digital experiences. Sometimes these digital experiences will take the form of interactions on or with the site or page. My interactions with Apple's website, for example, were definitely staged experiences. The website designers gave a lot of thought to what I'd do— how many choices I'd want, where I'd look, and how I would most likely click on a product. That was a staged experience.

Digital experience design also has a lot to do with being authentic online. You'll see that a full third of this book is devoted to the online community experience that many emerging social networking sites are providing, both to their customers as well as customer to customer. These sites will fail if they are perceived as inauthentic. Why? People want to connect with other real people and with companies that seem to care—about their product and about their customers.

What Experience Does for Customers

What does digital experience design do for customers, clients, or website visitors? Simply put, if it's memorable, they'll revisit. If it's easy to use, they'll use it again. If they have fun, they'll want to do it again. You should have at least three goals when designing digital experiences:

1. **Help visitors think about their own stuff.** They don't want to think about how many clicks it will take to get to the center of your website. They want to think about buying a laptop, connecting with Jim in Destin, or checking out that movie they heard about last week.

2. **Get visitors coming back for more.** Your main goal is *stickiness.* You want visitors staying on your site (or getting your stuff via feeds) and coming back again and again. You want them regularly visiting and interacting with each other. You want them buying stuff!

3. **Turn your site into their third space.** Ever heard the concept of third space? The "proliferation of BEING SPACES and BRAND SPACES ('commercial living-room-like settings in the public space, where catering and entertainment aren't just the main attraction, but are there to facilitate out-of-home, out-of-office activities like watching a movie, reading a book, meeting friends and colleagues, and so on') is making it easier than ever to leave domestic or office hassles behind."[6] Put simply, you and I are more likely to invest our time in a website that offers entertaining and social activities—a digital space that offers an engaging experience. You want your customers to spend lots of time on your site: interacting with you and others, selling your product for you, and, of course, buying. You want your website to be a third space for your customers and your website's visitors.

Ultimate Goal

No, your ultimate goal is not to sell T-shirts (if your company sells T-shirts). No, it's not to check out books (if you're a library). It's to enchant and captivate your users. Why? Because if you can figure out how to enchant and captivate your users, then the other parts (buying and checking out) will be easy. You will have turned those customers into evangelists, and your evangelists will do much of your marketing for you.

The rest of this book explains what it means to design a digital experience. Come along for the *experience*!

Endnotes

1. Silver Dollar City, www.bransonsilverdollarcity.com (accessed January 18, 2008).

2. Silver Dollar City, "About Us," www.bransonsilverdollarcity.com/aboutus (accessed January 18, 2008).

3. David Lee King, "i just bought a mac," flickr.com/photos/david king/431764463 (accessed January 18, 2008).

4. B. Joseph Pine II, "Escape the Commoditization Trap," *Forward* (May–June 2007): 52.

5. B. Joseph Pine II and James H. Gilmore, Create Economic Value with Engaging Experiences, Deluxe Knowledge Quarterly, first quarter 2004, www.strategichorizons.com/documents/DeluxeKnowledge-04Q1-CreatingEconomicValue.pdf (accessed January 22, 2008).

6. "TRANSUMERS: Consumers Driven by Experiences," Trendwatching, November 2006, www.trendwatching.com/trends/transumers.htm (accessed January 18, 2008).

PART I

Structural
Focus

CHAPTER
2

What Is Structural Focus?

Everything has a structure. The computer I'm typing on right now has a structure—the casing, the internal parts, even the software was created or built. The creation of all that complex structure took quite a bit of planning. How is this accomplished? Well, that's what the rest of this book is about. A well-designed digital experience begins with a solid structure. That structure needs to support the site being built, it needs to work well, and it needs to stay out of the user's way; it should be invisible to the visitor.

Physical space is a great metaphor for digital space, so let's begin by discussing architecture and the structural focus that exists when building and then comparing that structure to a digital space. We'll keep it simple—because I know little about constructing a building. Let's use building a house as our example.

Planning Before Building

When a house is built, construction workers don't simply show up with their tool belts, nails, and a bunch of wood and start randomly hammering and sawing away until a house magically appears. To avoid the chaos that would surely result, architects plan and design, usually far in advance of the construction workers' arrival at the building site.

Architects design a house by creating a plan. They start by checking out the building site before the actual construction begins. They need to find out whether the ground is level or whether they'll need to bulldoze. They also need to decide whether the house will have a raised foundation, a slab foundation, or a basement. Once they have surveyed the site, they have a good understanding of the unique challenges and opportunities of the environment.

Just as a house or building can be designed to provide a great experience for the homeowner or visitor, a website can be designed to provide a useful, pleasant, entertaining, or educational experience. The process used when building a house is somewhat similar to that used when building a website.

Successful web projects don't usually start by gathering a group of coders into a room full of computers and telling them to build something. Instead, before the web developers are given the website project, a "web architect" needs to create plans for the site. Someone has to decide what the website's focus should be, what features it should have, and how it should look. The web designers are given these plans and then build the website from the plans (also called *specifications*).

Choosing the Building Material

Back at our house project, the building contractor has a big job: turning the architect's plans into reality. The contractor examines the plans and makes sure the features the architect created on paper actually work in the real world. The building contractor also chooses the appropriate building materials and tools needed to complete the house. The contractor might even choose the construction workers.

On the web, the building contractor for our digital space is usually a web developer or team of developers. The developer or team also needs to choose the right tools for the job. For example, the choice of coding languages needs to be appropriate for the goal of the digital application or website. Sometimes, a PERL script will achieve the best, invisible, out-of-the-way experience. Sometimes, JavaScript and XML might provide the most seamless experience.

The Infrastructure

In a house, many internal systems need to be created. For example, electricity, heating and cooling, and plumbing systems need to be added. Those systems need to "just work" for the homeowner (i.e., the end user); they need to be easy to use. No one wants to give up leisure time because an internal system keeps breaking or because it's necessary to read a thick owner's manual to figure out how to use one of the internal systems.

In a website, servers are a highly important back-end infrastructure that can make or break an experience. Are you creating a large website with an application that will have many facets and that many people will be using? If so, make sure your project web servers are robust enough to handle lots of visitors. They also need to be ready to scale up as your website becomes popular.

The Experience

Now let's shift the focus of our house analogy to creating a positive experience for the person who purchases that house. When a pleasant experience is added to the design of the house, the result (hopefully) is a happy, satisfied homeowner—one who will recommend the builder to others.

In some cases, it's OK to make the experience invisible and unobtrusive for the user. With electricity, for instance, the goal is to make sure the homeowners don't have to think about electricity. If they're flipping on a light, they just want light. They don't want to have to think about things such as breakers or which way to flip the switch; in other words, the experience should be immediately useful and usable.

Larger or commercial buildings need a logical flow in traffic areas, and the building planner needs to think about where people will go when entering the building. If a bank is being designed, a customer might want to go directly to the teller counter, so the teller needs to be immediately visible and accessible. Signage might need to be created that clearly directs the customer to different banking services. The bank customer doesn't want to have to think, "OK, I'm in the bank—where do I go now? Who's that person? Where do I deposit my money?" Customers just want to complete their bank business and get on with their lives.

Did you know that some organizations hire people to help create signage in their buildings? These people are called *way finders*. Way finders plan all the directional helps in a building, including where signs will be placed, what they will look like, and the size they need to be.

Just as buildings have a plan for signage, your digital space needs logical, understandable signage. That means creating helpful information architecture. The web team needs to put some serious thought into directional structures such as page naming schemes, navigational elements, and the digital pathways your visitors will take to reach your main content areas. You may need to answer questions such as these: How do visitors get from point A to point B on your website? Does it make sense? Is it easy to get there? This shouldn't be only planned from your "front door" (the main page of your website) either; these directional elements need to be considered on every section of your site. Some of your customers will use your front door, but many others will find you through a search engine or will click on an emailed link from a friend. Make sure your navigation works great on your secondary pages as well as your main page.

The Icing on the Cake

Back in our metaphorical house, the appearance of things such as lighting, parking, color schemes, and bathrooms can be designed with an eye to a positive experience. The appearance of these things might not be the focal point of the homeowner's experience (how many times do homeowners really sit down and think, "Wow—I love my driveway!"). Then again, how many parties quickly become difficult when the parking is bad? That's why even the appearance of those secondary things need to be designed with an eye to the homeowner's experience.

When thinking about the structure of your digital space, you also have to give some serious thought to designing the look of the site. The web is, on the surface at least, a visual medium: It's something visitors view. Because of that, a digital space planner should make sure that what your customers see is attractive. Unfortunately, poorly designed visual aspects of a site will most definitely provide a negative customer experience. So please, no black backgrounds with reams of 9-point, white copy! By making sure your site's visual design is pleasing to a majority of your users, you will greatly improve their experience with it.

Finally, you need to make sure your digital space is actually usable. This is easily done with *usability* testing. There are entire books dedicated to website usability (although this isn't one of them). I recommend Steve Krug's book, *Don't Make Me Think: A Common Sense Approach to Web Usability.* Krug will show you how to do usability testing so that you can make sure the amazing digital space you just created actually works for your users.

Structure Is Experience

I hope I have managed to convey the idea that a well-designed digital experience should, in most cases, be invisible to the user. Think about it for a second. When you're at a cool restaurant and need to go to the restroom, your goal is not to be wowed by the naming scheme or sign placement of some way-finding expert. Your goal is to get to the restroom, and anything that makes it easy is positive. In your digital space, your customers want to do what they want to do and not be forced to think about what was in the website designer's head when the site was created.

So make sure your digital space's structure stays out of your customers' way. Yes, it should look good, but those good looks don't have to be obtrusive. The structure can be visually appealing yet still direct users immediately to the thing they came to your website to do. Try to design with that goal in mind.

Kathy Sierra, creator of the Creating Passionate Users blog, used an effective image to describe this concept in her post titled, "It's the [?], stupid!"[1] Her image focuses on the user experience through two visuals. The first is of a man sitting on a lawn chair with a laptop. His fist is raised high in the air, and he is saying, "I Rule!" The second visual is of a group of icons labeled "cool features." But we are told not to focus on the second image; we are told to focus on the first idea. Sierra explains, "That 'I Rule!' experience should drive what most of you are trying to build or promote. [Note for

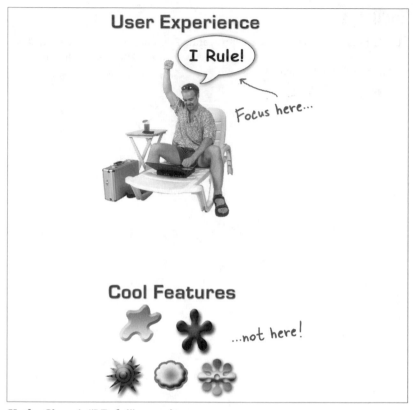

Kathy Sierra's "I Rule!" experience

clarification: We mean 'I Rule!' like that 'YES!' feeling you get when you do something tricky, *successfully*.]"[2]

Chapters 3 and 4 discuss ways to structure a digital experience by focusing on the nuts-and-bolts user experience or on a marketing-centered, experience-focused goal. We'll also take a look at information architecture and usability and see how they affect the digital experience.

Endnotes

1. Kathy Sierra, "It's the [?], stupid!" Creating Passionate Users, February 1, 2006, headrush.typepad.com/creating_passionate_users/2006/02/its_the_stupid.html (accessed January 24, 2008).

2. Sierra.

CHAPTER
3

Elements of Digital Experience Design

A successful customer experience is the goal, but it requires much preparation to attain. This chapter is for the site creator. It explains the nuts and bolts of designing user experiences— how programmers and designers help create digital experiences by the choices they make during the construction of the site.

This customer focus can be achieved in many ways. I will explain three very different models of building the user experience:

- Jesse James Garrett's *User Experience* model

- David Armano's *Experience Map* model

- 37signals' *Getting Real* model

In spite of their differing approaches, these models have the same goals: (1) to create a great customer experience, and (2) to get the organization's product, service, or message out to the organization's digital community. Let's take a look at each model.

Jesse James Garrett's *Elements of User Experience*

Jesse James Garrett first created a PDF file and then wrote a book, *The Elements of User Experience: User-Centered Design for the Web*, about designing a successful user experience. Instead of focusing

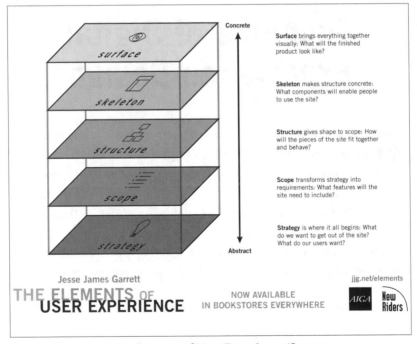

Jesse James Garrett's *Elements of User Experience* (Source: www.jjg.net/elements/pdf/elements.pdf)

on experiences one can provide to the user (the topic of this book), Garrett explores a structured process of digital creation—how web designers, programmers, and managers can successfully create a website that the customer finds useful.

Garrett has divided his process into five steps: strategy, scope, structure, skeleton, and surface.[1]

Strategy

The strategy phase of the project involves creating a road map that, in essence, will get you from the planning stages to the final product. Strategy focuses on two primary sets of needs: those of the user and those of the organization.

User needs always come first—after all, the goal of most websites is to attract customers. This step begins with figuring out what customers want. Why should people visit your site? Are you selling something they want? Will they want extra information to accompany a product—product descriptions, demonstrations of the product in action, or perhaps a customer-created review of the product and how it should be used? Will customers want to interact with you? Will they want to tell stories of how they use your product or service? These are just a few of the questions that should be answered in this phase.

How do you find out what your customers want to do on your website? Focus groups and surveys are a great way to start. A focus group is nothing more than a group of customers telling you what they want to do when they walk through your digital doors. Ask your focus group open-ended questions to discover these things.

Surveys are another great way to gather feedback about user needs. These can be sent out with a product, or you can link to them on your current website. Surveys don't have to be long; they can consist of five to 10 open-ended questions, such as, "What do you do when you visit our site?" or "What are three things you would change about our site?" With information gathered during these sessions, a web designer can start figuring out what customers like and don't like on your current site.

Website analytics are another good way to gather information about your customers. Statistics showing popular destinations on your site, for example, could point to something that a majority of your customers like. Then you can work on figuring out how to expand or emphasize that area. Another way to use website analytics is to look at search keywords. These show what words and phrases people entered in search engines (such as Google) to get to your website. Examine those words and phrases, and make sure the products or services behind those search terms are easy to find on your site.

Following closely behind user needs are organizational goals. What goals does your organization have? These should also be planned for during the strategy phase. What things do you want customers to see when they open your digital doors? What focus are you hoping to create? Are you planning to heavily market a new product or feature with this website? These organizational goals need to be incorporated into the building of the site. One good way to meet organizational goals is to look at the end result—what you hope will have happened a year from the release of the website. Figure out the short-range goals, then focus your site strategy on meeting them.

It's also important to mesh your organizational goals with your users' needs. If what you hope to do as an organization and what your user wants to do while visiting your site are two completely different things, then you (and your organization) have a problem. Make sure to keep in tune with your customers and their needs!

Scope

Once a solid strategy is clarified, an organization needs to create functional specifications for the project. This is called the scope. A scope is a descriptive document that explains, in as much detail as needed, what the site should do. It should answer questions such as the following:

- What are the goals of the site?

- What does the organization hope to accomplish with the site?

- What type of experience does the organization want to provide the customer?

- How should content be accessed?

The answers to these questions may not seem as if they have anything to do with the user's experience, but they really do. After thinking through, via the strategy step, what both users and the organization want to accomplish on this site, a site designer has a good (but undefined) idea of the site's goals. Defining functional requirements for those goals using a scope lays out the groundwork for everyone. It describes the site's goals and how you plan to meet them. Think of it as the narrative of the plan, or a description of what the plan should look like.

The scope is also a document that everyone should read and initial to indicate that everyone has read and understands the plan (well, it's supposed to work like that, anyway!) and agrees that it should be used as the blueprint. Because this is a written document, it allows you to look back later at a concise version of the plan that was agreed to originally.

Usually, the scope includes input from the various departments of your company. For example, marketing will add its bit about how the site will market a product or service and what it will supply to the finished site. Programmers will have a section describing their role—what they'll need to build the site and possibly even its planned functionality. And the information technology (IT) team will discuss such things as servers and storage space.

The scope should include a description of menu functionality (whether it should be a drop-down, whether it should move, etc.). It's also a great place to describe the different types of web pages needed and how many pages are needed for the site on "opening day." The idea is not to outline specific pages in detail but rather to describe what sections are needed on the site. For example, is an "About Us" section needed? If so, what information should be included on that page? Should customers have the ability to leave comments on the content in that section? Should RSS feeds be included? Each section needs to be described in this way.

Content requirements should be planned in the scope phase of the project, too. Although you don't have to have finished, finalized content at this early phase, you do have to know what content you want to provide and who will provide it. Make sure to include a summary and purpose for each part of the site.

For example, a small business selling a few products might need content for many parts of its site, including a description of each product, why someone should buy the product, what it will do for the customer, how to buy the product, a shopping cart purchasing section, a "My Account" section that stores customer information, a customer rating or review section, company information, a blog that covers new developments, a way to contact the company for more information, and perhaps a help or support section.

For each of these sections, the scope document should describe requirements. For example, when describing the product section, you might write that you need this type of content: a photo of each product, a brief description, one or two user reviews, user tags, a "people who bought this product also bought ..." section, pricing information, and a "get it now" button.

Structure

The next step of the project is structure. Here you create your plan for the presentation of information. The functionality of the interactions planned to take place on the site is also created here.

We'll discuss information architecture more in Chapter 4. For now, let's discuss some basics of information architecture that help provide a good digital experience for the user. When creating information architecture for a website, focus on planning the wording of labels and mapping out the content of the site in a logical way. Being sure that these words and phrases make sense to your customers and being consistent in the labels you use across different parts of the site will help.

For example, consistent menu labels will help customers move about effortlessly and will promote a positive experience on your website. If a certain section is labeled two or more ways in different parts of the site, that forces your customers to think about the website rather than the thing they hope to accomplish. You have, in essence, taken their eyes off the goal (to buy your product). Your goal should be to help your customers achieve their goal easily. Using consistent labels and labeling schemes will help.

Skeleton

After the first three steps are complete, you can finally start thinking about the look and feel of the website or web application—from the inside out. To start, you must build a skeleton on which to place the surface of the site.

During the skeleton phase of the project, the navigation and interface elements are designed. This is done by designing a *wireframe*, which is like a set of architectural blueprints. Instead of displaying the actual design and colors, a wireframe is merely an outline of the site. Essential elements of the site are placed in the wireframe and described.

Surface

All the preceding steps lead us to the surface of the site. Here your web designers can finally start filling in the site skeleton with a compelling visual design. Design considerations include the page elements, such as buttons and menus, as well as the content.

That's how Garrett's plan works. It's logical and linear. The goal is to move from the initial, broad planning phases to the more specific building phases and finally to the icing on the cake—visually designing the surface elements.

David Armano's *Experience Map*

This second way to build, or structure, a digital experience comes out of a marketing and design background. David Armano, of the blog Logic + Emotion, created and blogged about the *Experience Map*.[2] The *Experience Map* provides a great map to building experiences. It works hand-in-hand with Garrett's *User Experience* model. Whereas Garrett wrote mainly about structure, interaction, and usability, Armano's map starts a few steps back. Armano provides valuable insight into the beginning, discovery phases of the project and has broken his approach into five steps: uncover, define, ideate, build, and design.[3]

Uncover

First comes the uncover step. This step "starts with the customer, their wants, needs and expectations—the brand and business objectives are also articulated to ensure that the experience (yet to be determined) will be strategically aligned."[4]

The model begins, much as Garrett's model did, with customer and organization goals. Obviously, without customers, most websites fail. You can use many techniques to figure out what your customers want. Three techniques listed on the *Experience Map* are *personas/scenarios* (discussed in Chapter 11); *behavior mapping*, or observing what people do in a space or on a website and recording what happened on a plan of that space or site; and *shadowing*, or watching people interact with your website or application in their natural setting (their office, home, etc.).

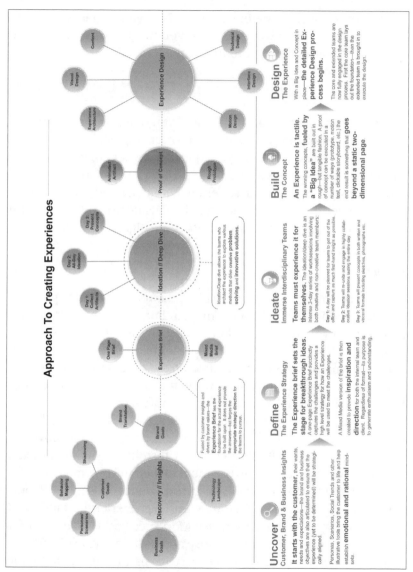

David Armano's *Experience Map* (Source: darmano.typepad.
com/.shared/image.html?/photos/uncategorized/experience_map.gif)

Also important are the business goals of your organization. Do you want to sell more widgets? Then you need to make sure those widgets are featured prominently on your website.

Define

In the definition phase of the project, you define your experience strategy and spell out what you want to accomplish. A great way to do this is to create a one-page "Experience Brief" that "succinctly captures the challenges and provides a high level strategy."[5] Create a short description of your experience strategy and how this new site will meet those experience needs. This document guides and inspires the team while it's working on the digital project.

Ideate

Next comes the ideation phase. This is the most "markety" phase of the *Experience Map* model, and I'm including it here mainly for completeness. But it can also, if done correctly, enhance the customer experience. During this phase, the digital team creating the experience is immersed in the experience of the product or service. The team members learn firsthand what the product or service does before they build a website for it. For example, if our team were building a website for the iPhone, a team leader would probably fill the team in on the details of the iPhone and perhaps even provide a demonstration. Then the leader might distribute iPhones to team members with instructions to use them to their full potential for a day or two; that would be immersion in the experience of using an iPhone. Immersion provides team members with a greater understanding of their website goals. The *Experience Map* specifies a 3-day plan for immersion and includes both creative and technical teams. Why? The goal of the ideation phase is to get everyone on the same boat for the project. The shared experience is a guide to help the team understand customer needs by experiencing those needs themselves.

Build

In the build step, the design team actually builds a prototype of the concept, if necessary. The prototype can be rough, but it needs to be good enough so that your idea gets across to whomever it is you're presenting the idea to—most likely customers, staff, or a client.

Design

Just as in Garrett's model, Armano places the design step dead last in the process—well, not quite last, because in this model you *did* build a proof or concept already. This last step continues the process of website creation into a final product: You finally add the actual functionality and interactions.

37signals' *Getting Real*

So far, we have examined two models of building a digital experience—both focused on the creation of the site—that provide a walk-through of the process, from the initial idea to the actual release date. The *Getting Real* model differs. The book *Getting Real*, by 37signals (www.37signals.com), a company that builds web-based applications, doesn't offer the nuts and bolts of building a digital experience; it focuses on parts and pieces of the digital experience, from problem solving to website creation. Let's explore the good advice 37signals has to offer on creating digital experiences.

Problem Solving

According to the 37signals authors, "When you solve your own problem, you create a tool that you're passionate about. And passion is key. Passion means you'll truly use it and care about it. And that's the best way to get others to feel passionate about it too."[6]

They emphasize that if you are passionate, it will show in the way you build your products and in the care you have taken with each part of them. The goal is to generate the same passionate interest in your customers.

Put another way, "You need to have a desire to tell the story. You need to be personally invested in some way."[7] The programmer should want to build the web application. That's harder to achieve; in many cases, programmers' work isn't so much about what they want as about what the company wants. If your programmers are just working for a paycheck, though, the authors of *Getting Real* think that's a bad state of operation. In fact, they feel that if the application doesn't excite you, then something must be wrong. Apathy shows up when your customer starts using the site or the application—the excitement, or lack thereof, will be readily apparent to the site's visitors and will certainly result in an experience, but perhaps just a mediocre or even negative one.

Scope

Remember the scope section in Garrett's model, which dealt with functional specification requirements? Here's what 37signals says about scope: "If you can't fit everything in within the time and budget allotted then don't expand the time and budget. Instead, pull back the scope. ... [L]aunching something great that's a little smaller in scope than planned is better than launching something mediocre and full of holes."[8] Instead of a traditional corporate model, in which more developers are added to a project to make deadline, sometimes pulling back is necessary.

Why? For starters, pulling back on project requirements allows the organization to treat its workers well. Fewer stressed-out developers mean fewer sloppy mistakes, which promotes a better building experience. The project with a smaller, more doable scope has a better chance of success because more thought and time were put into the parts that were released. The final product should provide a better experience for the user, which will keep customers coming back to see those "added features" later (the ones you didn't get to when you cut back the original scope).

Functional Specifications

The 37signals creators don't like rigid functional specifications. They suggest not writing a functional specifications document and also say: "An app is not real until builders are building it, designers are designing it, and people are using it. Functional specs are just words on paper."[9]

According to 37signals, creating a formal specifications document tends to slow down the creative process, especially in a large organization: "The more-mass company will likely still be discussing changes or pushing them through its bureaucratic process long after the less-mass company has made the switch."[10] Building without a functional specs list gives smaller companies an advantage if they're creating competitive products.

This approach varies from Garrett's steps of creating functional specs and then sticking to them. The authors of *Getting Real* explain, "Build, don't write. If you need to explain something, try mocking it up and prototyping it rather than writing a long-winded document."[11] In the 37signals model, you start by brainstorming, and then skip right ahead to the design phase of the project. 37signals suggests four steps for designing a website or a web application:

1. **Brainstorm** creative ideas about the product or website (loosely similar to the scope section in Garrett's model).

2. **Make paper sketches**. The goal here is to convert the concepts created during brainstorming into rough drafts of designs (similar to the skeleton step in Garrett's plan).

3. **Create HTML screens**. Build a real-time prototype. No programming happens yet—it's all just HTML and CSS

[cascading style sheets] so people can see what the real thing will look like.

4. **Code it**. This is the final step. When your mock-up looks good and demonstrates enough of the necessary functionality, go ahead and plug in the programming code.[12]

This should be a fast process. The goal is to launch your new product or website to customers, right? The goal is to get it done quickly, even if it's a bit rough around the edges. Then your customers have time to experience the new site or application, see what they like and don't like, and suggest improvements. This is a very community-driven way to work because it allows the organization to do the bulk of the work at the beginning without any interruptions and then allows the fine-tuning to be driven by customers. This provides your customers with a great experience (assuming you do a good job, of course).

If, for some reason, you have to write a directional document about the site or application you're getting ready to build, don't write a detailed functional specification document, because according to 37signals authors, such specifications can force you into making important decisions when you have very little information. Instead, be a little creative and write a story! The story should be short—one page at the most. And instead of focusing on interface design details, focus on the story—on what the site or application needs to do. Stick to the experience rather than getting bogged down in details. Focus on strategy rather than on tactics. If you're thinking about the customer's experience from the start of your project, you'll be more likely to provide the experience you were thinking about in the beginning.

Interface Design First

While the *User Experience* and *Experience Map* models place interface design toward the latter part of the project, the *Getting Real* model suggests building the interface first. Why? When people visit a site, according to 37signals, they're not thinking, "Look at this AJAX library they used. How cool is that?" Instead, visitors are thinking, "This site looks good. I'll land here for a while and see what gives." This is an important concept in digital experience design: "The interface is your product ... [What] people see is what you're selling."[13] The visual interface is your product's image, and you will send potential customers away if you get the interface wrong.

Remember Garrett's structure step, where building important functionality begins? The writers at 37signals suggest a similar idea in a slightly different way: starting at the epicenter and designing the most important content first. Whatever the page absolutely can't live without is the epicenter. So when designing a blog, for example, the epicenter would be the individual blog post: how the text looks, how graphics are wrapped around the text, and font colors and styles. On the website of a large nonprofit, the epicenter might be the organization's services and, potentially, its story—the content on a page. For a large software company, the epicenter would probably be the product pages and the customer's shopping cart (not your support pages!). Start by designing the most important content first, and then work out toward the edges.

Simplification

"Solve the simple problems and leave the hairy, difficult, nasty problems to everyone else."[14] With this insight, 37signals' authors sum up something that holds true for many Web 2.0 products (this concept is discussed in detail in Chapter 6). Most of their users neither want nor use advanced, I-might-use-this-once-a-year, complicated features. Instead, most users tend to use the default, basic features of most products and tools.

This idea of simplification is similar for most Web 2.0 sites. For example, a web-based word processor might include mainly basic desktop publishing features, such as the ability to make bold, italic, and underlined text, change font styles, and create a basic table, and that's OK. People who are using such a site might want simply to type and collaborate, and that tool allows them to do those two things quickly and simply. A good web-based word processor provides a good digital experience for the users by getting out of their way so that they don't have to think about advanced tool functionality.

In its own words, 37signals "looked at competitors, and discovered that project management isn't about charts, graphs, reports and statistics—it's about communication."[15] It discovered what its potential customers wanted to do with a web-based project management application, and it focused on creating a simple "I can do this" experience for them.

Simplification also provides a great experience for the developer (which again will provide a better experience for the users). 37signals realized that its developers sometimes spent large chunks of time on issues that didn't really matter, and that productivity could be much higher if that work was eliminated. So 37signals worked on honing its focus to the core of its product and then focused on building the best experience it could for that core (in its case, a simple-to-use project management tool).

Sometimes, simplification does not involve programming; it involves taking a simpler route you might have overlooked. "Search for detours around writing more software. Can you change the copy on the screen so that it suggests an alternate route to customers that doesn't require a change in the software model? For example, can you suggest that people upload images of a specific size instead of doing the image manipulation on the server side?"[16] This type of thinking allows the developers to stay focused on the primary goal of the project and to put most of their energy on that development instead of focusing on all the difficult-to-program rabbit trails that can appear in the life of a project. Simplification also helps keep developers passionate about the project by keeping the momentum of the project moving forward, which, in turn, will help provide customers a great experience because that passion will show in the final product.

So, you have just been introduced to the three different, yet complementary, models of user experience design. Which one should you use? There are no easy answers here—it will be different for each company or organization. You might follow one model closely or use aspects of all three. Figure out what your organization's needs are, and then choose the most appropriate path to help meet those needs.

Endnotes

1. Jesse James Garrett, "Elements of User Experience," March 30, 2000, www.jjg.net/ia/elements.pdf (accessed January 25, 2008).

2. David Armano, "Experience Map?," Logic + Emotion, darmano.typepad.com/logic_emotion/2006/04/experience_map.html (accessed January 25, 2008).

3. Armano.

4. Armano.

5. Armano.

6. 37signals, *Getting Real: The Smarter, Faster, Easier Way to Build a Successful Web Application*, 2006, 14. (The PDF version is available in a variety of formats at gettingreal.37signals.com.)

7. 37signals, 16

8. 37signals, 19.

9. 37signals, 115

10. 37signals, 28.

11. 37signals, 118.

12. 37signals, 64–65.

13. 37signals, 92.

14. 37signals, 13.

15. 37signals, 21.

16. 37signals, 106.

Information Architecture and Usability: Experience-Focused Design

What's the use of a refrigerator that's sealed on all four sides? There may be great food inside, but without a door providing access, it might as well be empty. In many ways, a website that's difficult to navigate is like that doorless refrigerator—users who can't get to the goods easily will likely seek out another source.

Information architecture and usability are usually discussed in terms of user experience and functionality: trying to make the website function correctly and trying to interest users in the site by making it usable and by labeling things correctly.

But I think there's more to information architecture than just labeling a site correctly and more to usability than simply checking to see whether links work correctly. Web designers should facilitate an experience in which users can quickly "get the goods." This chapter explores the experience design elements of both information architecture and usability.

Experience Elements of Information Architecture

Let's start by defining information architecture (IA). Wikipedia defines it simply as "the art and science of expressing a model or concept for information."[1] In *Information Architecture for the World Wide Web: Designing Large-Scale Web Sites*, Louis Rosenfeld and Peter Morville provide several more-detailed definitions:[2]

- "The structural design of shared information environments"

- "Combination of organization, labeling, search, and navigation systems within websites and intranets"

- "Art and science of shaping information products and experiences to support usability and findability"

- "An emerging discipline and community of practice focused on bringing principles of design and architecture to the digital landscape"

On the basis of these definitions, we may say that IA is the practice of applying structure to the information we create for websites.

According to Rosenfeld and Morville, four types of IA are represented on websites: searches, organization systems, labeling systems, and navigation systems.[3] Let's examine each one and then discuss the experience components of each.

Searches

Many websites incorporate search features throughout the site. But have you thought about how you can positively affect your users' search process on your website? Have you considered that visitors might be searching in different ways? Rosenfeld and Morville describe four user approaches to searching: [4]

- Exhaustive researching (when visitors are looking for everything pertaining to a particular subject or term)

- Exploratory seeking (when they're looking for only a few things)

- Finding the "right thing" (when they're looking for a specific item)

- Refinding (when they're hunting for something they've already found once but need again)

For each of these searches, visitors can be directed to different places that can help the search experience.

For example, Amazon.com provides many search features and options, depending on the customer's needs. A customer who needs to do exhaustive research has the option of searching for and finding a list of everything in Amazon.com's database. If doing exploratory seeking, the researcher can search a topic, look through some books, and browse through the "customers who bought this also bought" options to find other items of interest.

The customer can search via an ISBN or enter the whole title or author of a book when performing a very narrow search for the "right thing." And, if the customer needs to refind, Amazon.com has options to save items to a wish list for future browsing (and, as Amazon.com hopes, for purchasing).

Rosenfeld and Morville also say that when visiting a site, a customer wants to do one of three things: search, browse, or ask.[5] These behaviors extend to many websites (when hunting for information, anyway). Think about Home Depot's website for a second. When you visit the site, you are (1) looking for a particular thing

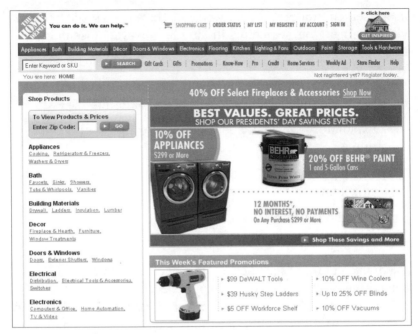

Home Depot's home page

you want to buy or for information about something (searching or browsing), (2) clicking around the site to get ideas about a project or a tool you're interested in (probably browsing), or (3) looking for an answer to a question, an email address, a customer service link, a help-me-now screen, or even a tip sheet on how to install something (asking).

One goal of IA is to make sure visitors to your site can do all these things (searching, browsing, and asking) easily on every page. Make it easy for them to find your "stuff" and to connect with someone if they need help. Add a link to a help screen or to your help-me-now feature if you are able to support one. These types of features help ensure that customers can use your site successfully.

Organization Systems

How do you organize the information presented on your website? There are many ways to organize, including arranging information in alphabetical, chronological, or geographical order. Which organizational style you use largely depends on your website's content and on the context in which that content resides.

You can have an experience mind-set here as well. Content should be arranged for the majority of your users. If the site is organized for the largest user group, then most of your site's customers are satisfied; the others can either learn your system or adapt as needed.

Home Depot does this by arranging its physical and digital content similarly. For example, when walking around a Home Depot store, you might notice that the shelves have large labels that state Tools or Paint. When browsing the Home Depot website, you will see the same organization system. This breeds familiarity—the physical and the digital worlds match, which allows customers to think about what they need to build a deck rather than about how to browse through the website to get to the section on building decks.

If you want more than one organization system on the same page, work to make the systems visually distinguishable. As Rosenfeld and Morville suggest, "In cases where multiple schemes must be presented on one page, you should communicate to designers the importance of preserving the integrity of each scheme."[6] And for each scheme, you want to have easy and transparent systems that allow users to think about *their* stuff rather than *your* stuff. Kathy Sierra puts it this way: "We don't want our users talking about the company or the product. All that matters is how they feel about themselves as a result of interacting with our product. How they feel about us has little impact on whether they'll become loyal (let alone passionate) users. All that matters is what we've helped them do or be."[7]

Labeling Systems

According to WordNet, a label is "a brief description given for pur-
poses of identification."[8] According to Rosenfeld and Morville,
labeling systems for web resources can include contextual links,
headings, navigation system choices, and index terms.[9]

Labeling on the web is extremely important. In fact, a confusing
label might turn users away. We don't want that! So what do we do?
Here are a few tips that will help provide good user experiences:

- Avoid jargon

- See what competitors are doing

- Ask your users

Catalog, materials, placing a hold, periodical databases, and
interlibrary loan: If these terms are familiar to you, you probably
love your local library! These are all examples of library jargon.
Library website designers have a hard job: They have to translate
library terms into friendlier terms for customers unfamiliar with
library lingo. At the same time, the designer has to make sure that
customers who *are* familiar with the jargon (and the services
behind the terms) can quickly find what they need. Most industries have jargon of their own that will be familiar to insiders but
confusing to others.

When creating labels for a website, make sure you're not using
company department names as labels or using internal slogans as
"helpful language" for your customers. These things may be
catchy, but they have the potential to confuse and irritate users if
the meaning isn't immediately evident.

In addition to avoiding jargon, it can be useful to study competitors' websites. Of course, you want your company's site to be
unique, but you may get some ideas for labeling systems that you
can use or adapt to your needs.

Finally, ask your users for suggestions. An easy way to learn how users approach the site is through card sorting. To use this method, write a list of web links on notecards and give them to customers to organize. Then have them tell you how they would label each pile they create. Look for trends or patterns in their labeling and use those labels on your site. This will be, in essence, a customer-generated organization system. By considering the needs of the customer first, you have taken a major step toward providing a successful customer experience.

Navigation Systems

Finally, let's talk a little about navigation systems on websites. There are many types of navigation systems, including global navigation systems (how the user gets around the whole site), local navigation systems (how the user gets around one page), and contextual navigation systems (navigation within the content of a page). In addition, many newer websites are building in tag cloud systems, visual navigation components, and popularity navigation elements.

One example of a navigation system "done right" is found on Target's website (www.target.com). Target has done a great job of creating an easy-to-use global navigation system for its website. At the site, this navigation system is found at the top of the page. Each link takes the customer to a different area of Target's online store. For example, clicking on "Women" finds women's clothes, clicking on "Kitchen" finds appliances and cookware, and clicking on "Electronics" finds cameras and console games.

Getting this global navigation system right—making it easy to understand and use—is essential to meeting a main goal for Target's website: selling products. If a customer can't navigate the site, it's guaranteed to result in a bad experience (and Target is guaranteed to lose a customer). Aim for high-level, seamless navigation that provides a great user experience.

Target's home page

Usability and Experience Design

A very important concept related to IA is usability. According to Wikipedia, the term is "used to denote the ease with which people can employ a particular tool or other human-made object in order to achieve a particular goal."[10] For websites, usability simply means how easy or difficult the site is to use. Usability is usually determined by asking questions about different parts of the website. Let's see how this concept relates to digital experience design.

Steve Krug, the author of *Don't Make Me Think: A Common Sense Approach to Web Usability,* asked his wife about difficult websites, and she responded that if she finds something hard to use, she won't use it as much. According to Krug, the job of digital experience providers "is to get rid of the question marks"[11] or, as Krug puts it in the title of his book, *Don't Make Me Think*. Remember, the goal for digital experience design is to allow visitors to your site to think about the things *they* want to think about rather than the functionality of the website.

Kathy Sierra found a unique way to sum up the essence of a successful website:

> The best user experiences are *enchanting*. They help the user enter an alternate reality, whether it's the world of making music, writing, sharing photos, coding, or managing a project. Even a spreadsheet has the potential to be as engaging as a game. Until the interface comes crashing into your virtual world, throwing you back to the real one. That intense feeling of being engaged—the flow state—is interrupted. The spell is broken.[12]

There are things you can do to make your website more usable. One of the most important is to put the "major things" on your main page. Make these important functions obvious and extremely easy to use. For example, if you are Wal-Mart, you should probably display products on the main page of your site as well as include obvious links to products. If you are a pizza place, you should probably have prices, menus, specials, and a way to order pizza online. A library should always provide a link to its online library catalog in a very visible location on the main page and offer one-click access to the catalog from each page of its site.

Figure out what questions your visitors are likely to have and answer those questions up front so that customers don't have to struggle with website functionality. Also provide an easy-to-see "what's this?" link so that your customers are able to find help quickly if they do have a problem. By incorporating these ideas,

Wal-Mart's home page

you will succeed in making a more usable website and provide a better experience for the customer.

Information Architecture, Usability, and Experience

Do you see how seemingly mundane concepts such as IA and usability are vital to the customer's digital experience? Design poorly (or don't think things through), and you'll provide a negative experience. Do you think that customer is coming back? Probably not. Do it correctly, and you should garner a loyal customer who will revisit your site repeatedly.

When you focus on the nuts and bolts of websites—the usability and the inner workings of your architecture—your customers will gain confidence in your service. It's sort of a "Sound Man Syndrome." At a concert or a worship service, when the audio engineer makes a mistake, *everyone* notices (usually it's accompanied by an ear-splitting *screech*). Afterwards the engineer gets a lot of feedback, all of it negative. But, if the engineer does a great job, what do you notice? Certainly not the engineer. You enjoy the great music or the speaker, without distraction.

It's the same with websites. Do your job well when it comes to usability and helpful information architecture, and your customers will be able to complete their business successfully, without distraction. You'll improve the digital experience on your website by anticipating potential problems before they occur. Positive experiences build the desire to return and to tell others about your site. And that means you have just turned a potential naysayer into an evangelist.

Endnotes

1. "Information architecture," Wikipedia: The Free Encyclopedia, en.wikipedia.org/wiki/Information_architecture (accessed May 9, 2007).

2. Louis Rosenfeld and Peter Morville, *Information Architecture for the World Wide Web: Designing Large-Scale Web Sites* (Portland, OR: O'Reilly Media, 2006), 4.

3. Rosenfeld and Morville, 14.

4. Rosenfeld and Morville, 34.

5. Rosenfeld and Morville, 35.

6. Rosenfeld and Morville, 68.

7. Kathy Sierra, "Reverse-engineering user reviews," Creating Passionate Users, headrush.typepad.com/creating_passionate_users/2007/01/reverse engineer.html (accessed July 3, 2007).

8. "Label," WordNet Search, wordnet.princeton.edu/perl/webwn?s=label (accessed July 3, 2007).

9. Rosenfeld and Morville, 86.

10. "Usability," Wikipedia: The Free Encyclopedia, en.wikipedia.org/wiki/Usability (accessed May 9, 2007).

11. Steve Krug, *Don't Make Me Think: A Common Sense Approach to Web Usability*, 2nd ed. (Berkeley, CA: New Riders Publishing, 2006), 9, 13.

12. Kathy Sierra, "User enchantment ....," Creating Passionate Users, March 15, 2006, headrush.typepad.com/creating_passionate_users/2006/03/user_enchantmen.html (accessed July 3, 2007).

PART 2 Community Focus

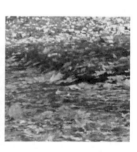

What Is Community Focus?

What exactly is community focus, and how does it facilitate experiences in the digital space? To answer these questions, let's consider what community focus means in the context of physical spaces, such as in a town hall meeting. In such meetings, people are focusing on one another: listening, sharing opinions, and discussing community needs. This type of interaction allows community members to voice opinions and concerns, providing a voice for the community. In this context, we can say community focus is an emphasis on participants' ideas, concerns, and interactions.

The town hall meeting is just one example; people obviously hold many different types of meetings, from religious gatherings to departmental business meetings to family reunions. We tend to think meetings are important. Why is that? Because we find conversation important, and meeting together facilitates conversation.

Conversation inherently facilitates something else, too. It allows us to interact with members of our community with whom we wouldn't normally interact or even know. This type of interaction allows us to feel as if we are participating in the "grand scheme of things." The challenge, then, is to usher community into our digital space.

Example from a Public Library

I work at Topeka & Shawnee County Public Library (TSCPL; www.tscpl.org), a large urban public library in the Midwest. In our physical space, the library is all about conversation, participation, sharing, and community. We hold thousands of meetings and events each year. Our parking lot is almost always packed, with some people visiting the library for books or web access and others visiting to attend a meeting.

The library has turned itself into a physical gathering place. People come to meet together or to learn something new from a famous author such as Ray Bradbury, and they come informally to hang out together at the cafe, the teen space, or around computers.

What's going on during these different meetings? Conversations are taking place: traditional conversations, formal "listen to the speaker" conversations, and question-and-answer types of conversations. There are discussions during breaks and jokes over a cup of coffee. And, of course, there are reference questions and requests for help finding information. In all these different types of interactions, conversation is front and center.

All this conversation and interaction can simply be called participation. This includes participation in conversations and participation in a meeting or another type of event (e.g., the square dancing class my kids and wife attended). It even includes participation by simply being there—it's all about participation.

TSCPL is a great example of community focus because it invites the community in to hold conversations, to interact with staff and with each other, and to participate. We want to include all these wonderful community elements in our digital space, too. By the time you read this sentence, we will have already created Phase 1 of our fledgling "digital branch." Or if we haven't, I'm in big trouble :-)

Digital Interaction

In a physical setting, conversation happens when two or more people interact. Digital conversation is similar. In a digital conversation, some form of digital interaction takes place. There are at least two basic types of digital interaction: interacting with an online tool and interacting with a person.

Tool Interaction

When visiting a website, you have to interact with it. You have to click on the links, examine the site to figure out how the navigation works, find the Play button to watch a video, and so on. Visiting a website isn't a passive activity—it's active, requiring you to actually do something.

That's the website as a whole. What about the site's smaller parts and pieces, such as filling out an online form? You are interacting with that form. Let's say you are signing up to join an online discussion group. Before you get to the actual group, you have to interact with the tool (the form). For example, you might need to:

- Type (interact with the computer to fill out the web form)

- Sign up for an account

- Understand what the menus and form boxes are for

- Know what to put in each text box of the form

Person Interaction via Commenting

The goal, of course, isn't simply to successfully interact with the web form but to interact with the community that's behind the form. In many cases, the digital tools we interact with are enabling community in the digital space. To understand what I mean, let's look at a few simple tools in general terms and then look at Amazon.com and eBay to see how we use these tools and sites to enable community, and, therefore, a community-focused experience.

Comment boxes abound in today's web world. They're everywhere, from digital versions of the complaint department to blog comment boxes to feedback mechanisms on social networking sites such as Flickr and YouTube. Even newspaper stories on global news sites such as the BBC and CNN now invite reader comment.

Is the goal here to interact with the comment form? Well, yes, in a basic sense. But the real goal of using these comment boxes is to enable a new form of community via conversation. In the same way that people used to be able to talk about a newspaper article in the barbershop while getting their hair cut, comment boxes now allow individuals to share thoughts and opinions with anyone interested in the article or the topic or the video.

There are two huge differences between those barbershop conversations and the conversations taking place in digital spaces. One difference is that in the old days, my comments in the barbershop were shared with two or three people—only those within hearing distance (and who were interested in the conversation). Now, my conversation starter has the potential to "go global." The whole world (well, the world that can connect to the web) can take part in my conversation.

The second difference is one of longevity. The barbershop conversations began and ended in the barbershop. If the topic was extremely interesting, the conversation might spread to others outside the shop, but for the most part, the conversation would have died when everyone taking part in the discussion left the building. This has changed in the digital age. The conversation I take part in when I comment on a news story, for example, theoretically never disappears (unless the site disappears or the webmaster deletes the database where my conversation is stored). Instead, my conversation is saved with the news story, and it can be accessed by anyone. It can be read today; it can be read (and commented on) 10 years from now. Theoretically, conversations I start today in the digital space can outlive me!

The conversation I started in the digital space can also be connected back to me. Comment forms usually include the option to point back to myself—by linking back to my email, my blog, or even my Flickr account (the norm in Flickr comments). That allows people interested in my thoughts to contact me personally to continue the conversation privately, even if the bulk of the conversation has stopped growing.

Tagging Starts Conversation

Tagging, or the process of creating a folksonomy, allows a unique type of community focus. What is tagging? Emerging web tools and services allow users to "tag" stuff—to assign a personally relevant keyword to something, such as blog posts, emails, web links, videos, or images. This is a way for someone to remember what an item was and to help them find it later or classify it. These tags also allow a new form of community-focused experience by way of community memory.

For example, when the New York subway workers went on strike (December 20–22, 2005), you could visit Flickr to see a part of the story you didn't get to see through traditional media. Traditional media told you what the strike was about, why it was happening, and what that meant for the daily commute to work. But Flickr told the story visually through images of closed subway stations, people walking across bridges to work, and signs in shop windows commiserating with fellow New Yorkers.

These visual stories of people's travel to work were told through the actual photos and were found and collected via the tags people assigned to those photos. That week, Flickr's hot tags and most popular tags included *nyctransitstrike*, *transitstrike2005*, and *transitstrike*. These tags created a viewable digital memory that was both findable and sharable. This is an important aspect of digital community: the ability to share experiences with others who are going through the same thing or who may be interested in the situation.

Mashing Up Digital Conversations

Mashups provide the same type of "extra awarded" experience and participation that tagging and commenting provide. Here's an example to get us started. Google Maps is an intuitive, useful online map application. Another site can create a database of area gas stations with current gas prices and put that database on the web—another helpful tool. But when those two tools, the gas station database and the map application, are combined, something special can happen. In this case, we suddenly have a visual map of the least expensive local gas stations that gets updated by members of the local community. That's a mashup.

Our gas prices mashup has created a special digital form of community experience: Through sharing, individuals are working together to cope with high gas prices. Mashups, in other words, can help organize the community in the physical space by allowing interaction in the digital space.

These examples (commenting, tagging, and creating mashups) facilitate participation in the digital space via conversation. This conversation—this participation and interaction—is the ticket to a community focus in digital experience. Participation and interaction

LosAngelesGasPrices.com

connect you to others, thus changing the experience from one of simply interacting with a tool to using the tool to interact with and connect with people.

Amazon.com's Community-Focused Experience

Let's look at another example of community-focused digital experience. Amazon.com has a cool tool that allows anyone to provide a product review and also allows users to rate those reviews, which started with the bookstore (every book can be reviewed by any customer). This ability provides customers with a powerful voice that may affect the purchases of other customers.

While reading one review can be interesting (depending on the source), the ability to read 100 reviews of a single book is what really turns these reviews into a community-focused experience. Reading numerous book reviews provides a glimpse into what the majority of readers think of the book. When an unfamiliar author writes a book that sounds interesting, you can find that book on Amazon.com and read what other people thought of it, a feature I find more useful than the book's marketing copy and one that allows me to form a more knowledgeable opinion. Having quick access to these customer-created book reviews allows you to tap into the collective wisdom of Amazon.com's reading community to see whether you might like the book. That's a powerful ability that didn't exist before the web.

But you don't have to stop there. You can also rate each review. This gives you the opportunity to point out the extreme reviews—either positive or negative. This customer review process ultimately allows for better information gathering because you can

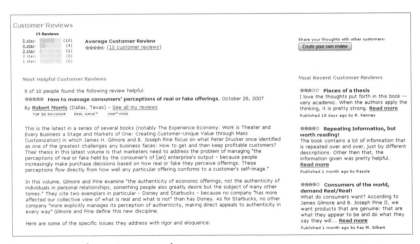

Amazon.com's customer review

find good reviews and good reviewers. It also lets you gather more levels of information: information about the book, information in the reviews, other reviewers' opinions of the review, and information on the reviewers themselves.

This deeper level of digging through reviews and reviewers provides an amazing digital experience—one of interaction and participation. It provides multiple doors of entry into the digital community:

- You can be passive and simply read the reviews. Here, you are passively participating in digital community simply by showing up, much like the crowd at a baseball game.

- You can go one further and rate a review. From here, all participation is active.

- You can read the book and then write your own review.

Participation

While Chapter 6 is devoted to participation, it also needs to be mentioned here because participation is extremely important in providing experience in a community-focused digital space.

Participation is about getting beyond the tool to the thing you want to do. When filling out a comment box, the user's goal isn't to successfully type words in the box and find and press the Send key. (Of course, that's certainly one small goal in the whole process, so you do want your form to be usable.) The big goal when filling out a comment form is to actually participate in a discussion. The reason people enter text in that comment box is because the thing they just read or watched made them think. Maybe it got their dander up, or they thought it was the most amazing thing they ever read. They want to add their thoughts to the mix: to participate. By having a comment box, you are inviting people to participate, in essence telling them, "I want you to add your thoughts. I want you to continue the conversation."

Ann Arbor (MI) District Library's website (www.aadl.org) uses the Drupal open source content management system, which allows visitors to comment on most pages of the site. In fact, it effectively turns most of the website into blogs, one of which is the library director's blog.

One day, the library director posted on what I would consider a ho-hum topic: a request for proposal (RFP) for a library building, a "we're going out for a bid" post. She received, when I last checked, 29 comments on that blog post—a post talking about a building plan on a library director's blog. That's just amazing. The system allowed community members to add their thoughts to the original post, in effect allowing the community to hold a conversation about the building project. It gave the commenters a voice.

Placing the post on the website, allowing people to subscribe to it via RSS, and allowing community members to add their thoughts via commenting helps make the library much more open and transparent to the general public than before.

Commenting opens up a new model for communication. Think about it: In the old, pre-web world, how did this RFP information reach the library's community? The library director would probably have written a couple paragraphs about the RFP, and then she would have sent that document to her marketing department. Marketing would have turned that document into a press release and sent it to the local media. Then, if it was a slow news day, maybe the local newspaper would have printed the press release in the community section of the newspaper.

That's how you, a library customer, might have discovered the information. How would you have responded and participated if you wanted to share your thoughts? You might have written or called the library—but honestly, not many people would. You might have sent in an editorial to the newspaper, which would then be edited for length and included in the editorial section (but

Ann Arbor District Library's comments page

only if there were enough room and only if the editor thought your comment was worthy of being included).

The new model trumps the old. You can now instantly add your thoughts to the conversation without much work or crossing of fingers. Simply visit a particular page, type in the comment box, and press the Send button: Your thoughts are added to the discussion.

Furthermore, your thoughts can receive immediate feedback, instead of the weeks required in the old model (and that's only if your letter to the editor was published). Participating digitally provides a wonderful way to connect to your community. It provides the sense of purpose and closeness of a town hall meeting, if you will—one that you can attend anytime, even at 2 AM.

Twitter and Community

One of the newer participatory Web 2.0 tools is the microblogging site Twitter (www.twitter.com). Twitter users can post comments or thoughts (up to 140 characters), sort of like sending an SMS (Short Message Service, which allows mobile device users to send and receive short text-based messages). The difference is that others can subscribe to your Twitter "Tweets." So Twitter's model is more of a bloglike, one-to-many, sharing model of communication rather than the one-to-one mode used in SMS messaging.

Scoble's Twitter page

Robert Scoble, a popular technology blogger, writer, and video-grapher, has a Twitter account. He announced on his blog that he was playing with Twitter and quickly amassed more than 4,000 Twitter followers. He was able to use his large Twitter following in some interesting ways. He has, of course, done the usual Twitter thing, telling everyone what he was doing (e.g., "I'm eating lunch with my kid."). But he has also used Twitter as a community brain, which has been fascinating to watch. He has asked his 4,000 Twitter readers questions and received instant feedback. He has been able to get a snapshot of the thinking of techie colleagues simply by posting a quick question and having potentially 4,000 immediate responses. Using Twitter in this way provided a great level of participation in the digital community created around Scoble's Twitter account and provided Scoble with an amazing digital experience—one of connecting and interacting with many.

Digital Experience

What are the types of digital experience to be had when one focuses on community? There are many, including the following:

- Real conversations

- Telling your personal stories

- Continuing the story

Real conversations take place in digital spaces. This can happen in a variety of ways, including commenting on blogs and other areas of a website, or through services such as instant messaging (IM) or microblogging sites such as Twitter. An online forum accessible to both site developers and customers is another way to hold conversations.

The goal, and sometimes the challenge, of conversation in digital spaces is to allow your customers to connect with you and with others. Connecting with the developer or the organization is important. Your customers want to interact with you. They want to know more about a product or a service. They want to have input on new website features, and they want to feel as if they know you and your product. They want to connect with you!

They also want to connect with each other. Company-produced product information is good, but what your customers *really* want to know is how 100 other customers have been using your product or service. They want to hear from "real people" what works, what doesn't, and how to get around that really odd usability issue that the developers simply didn't notice (and are now working furiously to correct). Amazon.com customer reviews are a great example of this and are a popular service for all of Amazon.com's many products.

Another digital experience provided is one of telling your personal stories. Michael Stephens, a library and information science professor at Dominican University, in River Forest, Illinois, really understands the power of story: "One way for libraries to promote their value and relevance is to tell the library's story every chance you get. Beyond daunting columns of statistics, users—and staff—might benefit from a story about how the library helped its users today. Ponder a staff exchange where internal stories can be told via a wiki or Weblog. You may find a lot of answers to the question: Why are we doing this?"[1]

What's so important about telling stories? Well, people want to know the history of your service and your company. They want to know why you developed it. They want to know who *you* are: what your credentials are, what else you've developed, whether you like using the product, and what shortcuts you take when using it. And they want to know all these things about others in the community, too. This helps connect people to one other—that community thing again. Statistics and numbers can show the same information, but stories are more memorable and will connect with a majority of your users much faster than mere sales figures do. That's why businesses use testimonials.

But people also want to participate in the story. They want to feel as if they are part of the story, as if they are the next chapter. This happens currently in Second Life (www.secondlife.com), a virtual world that allows people to participate in the story by building their mansion, changing their character's appearance, or joining a digital community and helping create that community. And your organization's presence in Second Life allows you to be part of your potential customer's story.

Flickr also allows you to participate visually in the story. Remember the New York subway strike I mentioned earlier? Everyone who took pictures and tagged them participated in the story of the strike and told a snippet of the story of their life—they told their personal story of dealing with the strike by documenting their walk to work. Combined, those contributions told a unique group story made up of unique individual stories.

People want to continue the story. The people affected by Hurricane Katrina had one story to tell: the actual hurricane and the immediate aftermath. But then that story continued: when they revisited their houses, when they received a FEMA trailer to live in, when they were able to rebuild their houses—even now, some have yet to reach that chapter of their story. And others can add to the story, too. I did, in fact, when I traveled with my kids and others from our church to the Mississippi coast a year after the hurricane to help with cleanup. So, even though I wasn't directly affected by the hurricane, I was able to tell my story in photos on Flickr showing the people I met, how the devastated coast looked, and how many houses remained unlivable a year later. I was able to add to the continuing Hurricane Katrina story.

Endnotes

1. Michael Stephens, "Telling the Library's Story: A TTW Fave," Tame the Web, tametheweb.com/2007/09/telling_the_librarys_story_a_t.html (accessed January 29, 2008).

CHAPTER
6

Emerging Tools for the Digital Community

Creating a digital community with unique experiences stemming from that community is a new concept. The possibilities intrigue me so much that I was inspired to write this book! Participating in today's digital community landscape involves the use of digital tools that either didn't exist 5 years ago or weren't accessible to nontechies. Much of the current change centers around Web 2.0 tools. Let's slow down for a minute and define some of these tools.

Tim O'Reilly, one of the people responsible for creating the term *Web 2.0*, has written, "Web 2.0 is the business revolution in the computer industry caused by the move to the Internet as platform, and an attempt to understand the rules for success on that new platform. Chief among those rules is this: Build applications that harness network effects to get better the more people use them."[1]

Wikipedia defines Web 2.0 in this manner: "Web 2.0 is a term describing the trend in the use of World Wide Web technology and web design that aims to enhance creativity, information sharing, and, most notably, collaboration among users."[2]

And Richard McManus has this to say:

> Web 2.0 at its most basic is using services on the Web. Some examples: Gmail for email, Flickr for photo-management, RSS for news delivery, eBay for shopping, Amazon for buying books. That's why the Web is being called a platform—because all of these services are being built and used on the Web. Why Web 2.0 only now though—hasn't Amazon been around since 1995? Why yes, but it's taken until 2005 for broadband and web technology to catch up and reach a "tipping point"—the Web is fast becoming the platform of choice for developers, business, media, public services, and so on.[3]

We can see that Web 2.0 as a concept is hard to define succinctly. The concept usually, though, involves ideas and terms such as *platform*, *social*, *communities*, and *strong user-generated component*. Though there are many Web 2.0 tools, they tend to have similarities. Web 2.0 tools usually include some combination of these components:

- **RSS feeds** – Ability to subscribe to content feeds

- **Commenting** – Ability to leave your thoughts on someone else's content

- **Tagging** – Ability to assign a personally relevant keyword to content (done by anyone, not just the content creator)

- **Reading RSS with feed readers** – Ability to retrieve and read the stuff you subscribe to

- **Mashups** – Ability to combine two or more things into something original

- **Web-based applications** (aka web as platform) – Ability to use web-based tools to do things, rather than using PC-based software to do things

- **User-generated content** – Ability to have the service's user community create content

- **A way to "friend" others** – Ability to designate users as friends or buddies

Web 2.0 has started something of an online revolution, affecting many people with broadband access. Individual industries are also starting to discover that their customers are using online tools, adding their own content to these tools and wanting to interact with each other and with the companies themselves. These industries have each created their own "2.0" moniker to describe what's going on in their fields (e.g., *Church 2.0*, *Media 2.0*, *Law 2.0*, and *Library 2.0*). Each of these subdivisions describes individual industries' attempt to figure out how to use 2.0 concepts in their niche communities.

These niche industries are dealing with 2.0 in at least two ways. First, they are beginning to incorporate 2.0 tools into their communities. One example of this would be a church starting a "what's happening this week" blog. Second, these industries are beginning to form new philosophies that stem from the openness and participation inherent in 2.0 services. For example, I'm involved with Library 2.0 in which librarians are trying to figure out what "always beta" means to a library (it might, for instance, mean that libraries have to continually rework services on the basis of changing customer needs and demographics).

Another example is the way the music industry is trying to deal with copyright issues in the digital age: a record company that wants to use digital rights management technology to keep unauthorized copies of songs to a minimum, while the band is giving away free music on its MySpace page. These examples don't deal with specific emerging tools. Instead, they show an overall philosophy of change.

Now that we have looked at some of the meanings and implications of Web 2.0 in general, let's take a look at the community experience aspects of blogs, wikis, Flickr, and videocasting.

Blogs

If blogs were people, they'd be the grandparents of Web 2.0 tools and services. Blogs (short for *weblogs*) were one of the earliest modes of using the web as a social tool; they incorporate writing, sharing thoughts, communicating, and commenting.

A blog is a kind of online hybrid of a newsletter and journal. The writer adds content at will, and the latest addition appears at the top of the continuous blog. Readers often have the ability to comment on the content but not to add new articles to the blog; only the blog owner has that ability.

Blogging software is basically a type of content management system created to make the tasks involved in blogging easier. This blog software allows blog posts to be tracked by date and by tag or category, allows the newest post to appear at the top of the page (reverse chronological order), and allows blog posts to be assigned multiple categories and tags.

Blogs provide a strong community-focused digital experience. That community-focused experience is found in the conversation itself. Blogs enable blog authors to share a little bit of themselves. Blogs allow readers to actively participate in the author's conversation. Blogs let the reader feel connected to the writer in the following ways, among others:

- **Familiarity with the author** – Usually blogs are written in a very personal style. Blog posts aren't usually edited, so whatever the blog author decides to write and publish ends up on the blog.

- **Commenting** – The ability to leave comments provides an opportunity for blog authors and their blog readers to connect. A reader thinks of a question or suggestion that can add to the conversation, and the author directly answers or responds, creating a conversation in the digital space of the blog. Authors also have the ability to comment on other people's blogs and to leave a link to their blog information, which creates another type of passive connection via trackbacks and pings.

- **Interest in the topic** – Readers' and writers' mutual interest in the topic also creates a type of connection. When both are interested in a topic and hold a conversation about that topic via writing a blog post and then commenting about the post, both author and reader have shared a connection in the digital world. If they ever meet in person, they can continue the conversation.

- **An interesting passive connection via RSS feeds** – When you subscribe to a feed, you can read the feed whenever you desire. The author has, in essence, sent the post to you.

The frequency of postings affects the blog experience. If the blog author posts just once a year, the feed subscriber will probably not feel very connected to the author. If the author only posts links to things he or she likes and doesn't add much text to those links, the reader will probably not experience much of a connection to the author. On the other hand, if that author posts a couple times a week, has interesting things to say, and allows his or her personality to shine through the blog posts, readers have the opportunity to get to "know" the author.

Wikis

A wiki is defined as "a medium which can be edited by anyone with access to it, and provides an easy method for linking from one page to another. Wikis are typically collaborative."[4] What a neat concept: Anyone can edit; anyone can participate. A good example of a wiki is Wikipedia. I believe we can observe at least two strong digital community experiences that wikis provide.

First, a wiki provides a sense of community input via collaboration, no matter the community. Because anyone can edit and add information to a wiki (depending on how the wiki is set up), people interested enough in the topic or community have the ability to add their own input. Then, because it's a community project and can be edited for clarity, the individual's personal writing style might disappear. On an active, growing wiki, someone else will probably edit out the personal but keep the factual. And that's fine because the goal of a wiki is collaboration and information sharing, not personal networking.

Second, a wiki provides an avenue for organic community growth. In fact, a wiki will grow in ways the wiki creator didn't expect. The successful wiki project will grow deeper as each wiki entry is tweaked and as more entries are added. The wiki becomes a bustling, growing community via visits, uses of content, additions, and edits.

Flickr

Flickr is a photo storage and sharing website that includes a social networking component. Once you have a Flickr account, you can do a number of things. You can upload photos to your account;

add tags, titles, and descriptions to each photo; and include metadata information on each photo, such as what camera you used, when you took the photo, and where you were geographically when you took it. Others can comment and leave notes on the photo. Depending on how your friends are set up, they can even add tags to your photos. Each Flickr account, and even each Flickr tag, has its own RSS feed.

You can also set up Flickr groups that create a multiuser grouping of photos. These groups can start discussions about the photos or the topic. Flickr even has basic email functionality so that you can connect with other Flickr users.

The community-focused experience with Flickr is similar to that of blogs, but Flickr has an added visual experience that is quite unique, as I alluded to in the last chapter. By subscribing to a person's photo feed, you get a glimpse of the person's life. For example, I broke my finger a few years ago and posted a picture of my cast. I received comments on that photo—words of sympathy, questions about what happened, and questions about how long I'd be wearing the cast. People felt enough of a connection that they responded to the photo.

Flickr also provides something to talk about when you see a Flickr friend in person. You might remember seeing his or her cast or new puppy and ask about it. You can discuss vacations with a visual of what your friend did already in your mind because you have seen it. It allows you to get past the surface ("Hey, want to see pics of my vacation?") to a deeper, more intimate level of conversation. You have already seen the vacation pictures. Now you can ask what the kids thought of that whale-watching tour.

Videocasting

Videocasting is sort of a combination of blogging and Flickr. Instead of typing or photographing your content, you video your topic and post those videos to your blog. A single video becomes a blog post. These videos can be anything from a series of shows (as Joanne Colan does on Rocketboom.com) to single creative projects (playing my dulcimer) to video experiments (using primarily text and music in a video format). Video in videoblogs usually serves as a way to communicate. Videobloggers want to start a discussion, share something they did, or even describe how they feel. The big difference between text-based blogs and videoblogs is this: Instead of telling something, the videoblogger has the opportunity to show something, through either demonstration or metaphor.

The community-focused experience of videoblogs is similar to blogs, wikis, and Flickr, but it is multisensory. In a videoblog post, the recipient can visually experience the content, much as one experiences a movie at the movie theater.

Personalities appear in videoblogs. In text, the goal may be to share something of interest in a personal way, but personality in text can be vague or minimal. Sometimes the personality that emerges from a blog doesn't seem to match up with the actual person. In fact, bloggers commonly misunderstand one another's tone or intent because of the limitations of text. In contrast, you actually see people with video. They are talking to you. You can read expression in their eyes, and you see them smile. You pick up on sarcasm visually and aurally (because you are listening as well), and you may even catch some inside jokes that appear as asides. Background music may add to the joke. These are things that can't be included in a textual format.

Personality appears passively through the videoblogger's choice of editing techniques, through background music tracks, and through certain types of filming. For example, in the Ze Frank show (a popular daily videoblog that ran every day in 2005–2006 at www.zefrank.com), Ze Frank always filmed close-ups of his face. It was intimate, as if you were sitting at a table with him and he was telling you his latest joke. His personality showed via his filming technique and his choice of quirky edits. Because of this (and because he was extremely funny and witty), he created a huge following and a community around those daily videoposts.

As we have seen, you can experience a digital community through reading, perusing photos, and watching videos. Community members might think they only have a loose connection to the people they meet in these digital worlds, but in actuality, they have shared thoughts, feelings, and experiences. You find out about their lives, and they find out about yours. You find out about their likes and dislikes. You learn from them and teach them. You converse with them in many ways. They send you their photos, their letters, and their vacation videos. They create something and give you permission to do so, too. A digital community is formed.

Endnotes

1. Tim O'Reilly, "Web 2.0 Compact Definition: Trying Again," O'Reilly Radar, radar.oreilly.com/archives/2006/12/web_20_compact.html (accessed September 30, 2007).

2. "Web 2.0," Wikipedia: The Free Encyclopedia, en.wikipedia.org/wiki/Web_2.0 (accessed July 16, 2008).

3. Richard McManus, "Web 2.0 Elevator Pitch," ReadWriteWeb, www.read writeweb.com/archives/web_20_elevator.php (accessed September 30, 2007).

4. "Wiki." Wikipedia: The Free Encyclopedia, en.wikipedia.org/wiki/Wiki (accessed October 3, 2007).

CHAPTER
7

Community Building Through Invitation

When I was a kid, my best friend lived down the street; his name was Jimmy Carter. (No, not former President Jimmy Carter—I'm not even sure if he liked peanuts.) Almost every single day, Jimmy or I would walk to the other's house, knock on the door, and ask this question (usually of the other's parent): "Can Jimmy (or David) come out and play?" Who knew that 30 years later, I'd be using that question as an example in a book on designing digital experiences?

What was I doing when I asked for Jimmy? I was inviting my friend to participate in a fun activity (usually a game of "war" or bike riding). A great way to encourage community and connectedness in digital spaces is to invite people to participate with you, your community, and your organization. Asking seems like a simple thing, but you might be surprised at how many companies and organizations don't ask their customers to participate. This chapter

77

focuses on the concepts of invitation and participation found in the digital experience.

A Google search for *define: invitation* found this: "A request (spoken or written) to participate or be present or take part in something; 'an invitation to lunch.'"[1] Here, *invitation* means to ask someone to do something with you. In our physical world, we invite others to do many things via asking. For example, we invite others to our birthday party or a social event; we are invited to join a club; a friend invites us to a concert or a ball game or church. All these invitations involve one or more people or organizations asking another or others to do something.

Furthermore, each of these invitations asks for a response, either positive (yes, count me in) or negative (no thanks, I can't come this weekend). The invitation is a foot in the door of a community. In fact, invitation is a very direct way to build community. By asking for new members or friends, for example, an invitation helps individuals become connected to a community and allows people to start becoming involved in the community. (There are cool digital invitations that we'll get to soon—just hang with me!)

For participation, I found two useful definitions. The first actually defined a synonym of participation: engagement, or "the act of sharing in the activities of a group."[2] The second definition (of *participation* per se) is "being actively involved in something."[3] So, participation can mean engagement (certainly in the way I'm talking about), and, of course, it can simply mean taking part in something. When we accept an invitation, the next step is participating, or engaging, in the activity.

Invitation and Participation in Digital Spaces

Now let's apply the concepts of invitation and participation to digital spaces. Here are two examples that illustrate what I mean by inviting participation. My first example goes back a couple of years to when I wrote the song *Are You Blogging This?* and created an accompanying video. I didn't realize it at the time, but that song invited a type of participation. Though I didn't ask anyone specifically to do anything, the title of my song apparently did. Once I posted it to YouTube and to my blog, people started responding to the invitation in the title of the song: In comments, in other blog posts—whenever it gets a mention—it's usually accompanied by someone telling me something like "Yes, David, I AM blogging this."[4]

My second example involves a blog post I made when I was having trouble with my blog. I directly asked readers to do two things for me: (1) Leave a comment if they saw my post, and (2) tell me what RSS reader they were using. And my awesome readers did! I received 45 comments answering my question. That post is a great example of an invitation to participate.[5]

There are two types of invitations in digital space: passive and active. When I posted *Are You Blogging This?* I didn't directly ask anyone to post anything about the song or to comment about it in my post. But the title of my song compelled viewers to participate because it asked a question. That's a good example of a passive invitation to participate. Passive invitations are indirect; they don't actually directly state "do this" or "read this." Instead, a passive invitation is more of an enabler, and it comes in at least two variations: content enablers and web tool enablers.

Content enablers make content compelling. They can do this in a variety of ways:

- Displaying content (text, video, photos)

- Creating compelling content

- Using action-oriented titles on posts

- Writing for the web by using a conversational tone in both writing and speaking (in video and podcasts)

- Including links with posts

Web tool enablers make content accessible and usable. They do this in the following ways:

- Allowing commenting

- Moderating promptly

- Always responding to comments

- Making sure content is easy to watch, listen to, or read

- Allowing multiple formats when possible (e.g., movies with accompanying text)

- Including RSS feeds

An active invitation is an easy concept to understand: It's simply asking your readers, viewers, or friends to participate in some way. A great example of active invitation was when I asked readers to leave a comment on my blog and tell me what RSS reader they were using.

Asking is an easy concept, but it can seem awkward when you first implement it into your writing or speaking style. It might help to think a little bit like a talk show host at a radio station. Talk show hosts continually invite participation. Flip on a morning show sometime and listen. You'll hear the host talk with the co-host about a topic for a minute or two and then ask listeners to call in and share their thoughts on the topic. Usually that invitation is repeated at various points during the show. Invitations via the web work in the following similar ways:

- If you ask once, a few people might notice and participate. If you ask frequently within a post, more people will notice and (hopefully) be willing to participate.

- Asking often can build momentum. People might not participate the first time they experience your digital space and your invitation. They might decide to sit back and lurk for a while. If you don't invite participation regularly, you won't get it. If you invite frequently, and your content and your invitations are engaging, you will slowly build a group of active participants in your digital space.

Now, let's look at participatory experiences in specific digital spaces: blogs, wikis, and social networking sites.

Invitations in Blogs

Blog-based invitations are a great place to start, because blogs can be amazing enablers of participation and engagement in either passive or active forms. Passive invitations in blogs can take many forms. One way is simply supplying an RSS feed with your blog. An RSS feed is an XML page of your content; in other words, a page arranged in such a way as to make the content easily readable in other formats. For example, you use an RSS feed to subscribe to a blog in an RSS reader. This way, you don't have to revisit the blog itself to check for content updates. Instead, when the blog author posts new content, you automatically receive the updates without having to do anything (that is, other than logging onto your RSS feed reader to check for updates). This might not seem terribly useful if you read only a couple of blogs, but if you read hundreds, then it's a huge time saver! I'm enabled to check for blog updates on my own time and read them in my own customized space.

Believe it or not, some blog owners don't automatically supply an RSS feed. For a time, blogs hosted on Blogger (www.blogger.com) didn't default to displaying a link to the blog's RSS feed. Blog owners need to make sure their RSS feed is displayed. Better yet, they should go one step further and make sure the RSS feed is displayed "above the fold"—probably in the upper right- or left-hand corner of the website. Bloggers can even use inviting language around the RSS feed link. For example, instead of using the words *RSS feed*, use *Subscribe* or *Subscribe to this blog*. Some blog tools let you create subscription buttons to popular RSS newsreaders, such as Google Reader or Bloglines. This way, it takes just a simple click to subscribe to a blog's content.

Good design is imperative in a passive invitation. If a site doesn't look good and isn't usable, people won't find the content compelling, either. Make sure to use easy-to-read fonts, provide a convenient printing option (through CSS or "Print this" buttons), and make it easy for users to leave comments.

Commenting is also essential to blogs—creating the blog post itself is only half the conversation; the comments create the other half. Simply allowing the ability to comment on a blog post is a form of passive participation. Even if you aren't directly asking for comments, you are opening up the possibility by providing the commenting tool to readers.

Some people like to moderate comments first, mainly to help fight spam or because the blog author has received a lot of off-topic or off-color comments in the past. Moderating is OK as long as comments are moderated quickly. Blogs, RSS, and comments allow a form of pretty immediate conversation to take place, and ignoring comment moderation duties for two weeks will kill the conversation.

Content can provide passive forms of invitation, too. For example, the titles used on blog posts can ask for participation. Consider my *Are You Blogging This?* example. The title was a question. So far I have received 62 comments on my blog and in YouTube—mostly people answering the question in the title.

Secondary types of content can also indirectly invite people to participate in interesting ways. For example, if you are discussing an organization, link to its website. Show pictures of the person or event. Link to other content on your blog so that people can get to know you better (familiarity breeds participation). My blog displays my latest comments, my popular posts, my Flickr feed, videos I've made, and even books I've read lately.

Now let's look at active invitations in blogs. There is one simple word to remember: *ask*. Ask readers to participate. Invite them to *do something*. You can ask for a number of things: a response (what do you think about this idea?), an action (send me your thoughts, click this link), or to come back for more of your fine content. You can even ask them to start participating by inviting them to subscribe to your RSS feed!

One good way to ask for participation is to figure out a goal for your post. What do you want people to do after reading? How about while they're reading? Figure out answers to those questions; then make sure to tell readers what it is you want them to do. One way to do this is to figure out the end result of your blog post and then write the post in a way that supports the end goal. Here are two examples of what I mean.

Topeka & Shawnee County Public Library has a blog. Last year, the blog writers created a 1-year series of posts (called 52 Questions) that asked participatory questions. Each weekly post introduced a topic, and each post asked for a response. This allowed readers to participate in an orderly way; it was directed participation.

Another example is the ReadWriteWeb (www.readwriteweb. com), a Web 2.0-focused emerging technology blog. The blog authors sometimes ask readers questions about what tools they use, getting a good informal poll of their readers. For example, they asked readers what blog reader they used and received a lot of answers. From that, the blog authors created a graph representing that use. They were able to get this response because they invited people to respond—they asked for it!

Invitations in Wikis

A wiki is a very different beast from a blog. You will remember that a wiki is "a collaborative website which can be directly edited by anyone with access to it."[6] Wikis obviously allow participation innately—that's what they're all about! But a wiki can work well or poorly, especially when it's made for use by a dispersed group. Let's explore passive and active invitations in wikis.

Passive invitation in wikis includes good wiki design and setting easy rules for the wiki. Good design will depend somewhat on the wiki software chosen. If you are creating a new wiki for a group, first ask the community members what types of wiki software they are familiar with. For example, if the community is used to using Wikipedia, you should consider using Mediawiki. Wikipedia uses Mediawiki software, so Wikipedia users are familiar with the way Mediawiki works.

Also, be sure that the goals for the wiki make sense. This step will involve some intense thinking beforehand: What do you want people to do on the wiki? Also, it involves writing good explanatory content about why the wiki exists and what participants should do using the wiki.

That relates to the next point: setting easy rules for the wiki. These rules should be stated succinctly and placed in a link near the top of the wiki. In addition to the goals for the wiki, you'll want to make sure there's a place for people to hold discussions about what changes need to be made or why a change was made. The wiki should also be easy to edit. If a password is needed, make sure it's easily accessible (either on the page itself or via an email to the administrator that is answered promptly). You will also want to allow comments wherever you possibly can. The goal of a wiki is collaboration, so you have to enable as much collaboration as possible within the wiki.

As for active forms of invitation on the wiki, you again need to ask for participation, and you need to create discussions about the wiki's content. Asking for participation can take place on the wiki, but it can also take place outside the wiki. Some examples of this include asking for participation in a discussion group, emailing people you know might be interested in the wiki, or posting invitations to participate on your organization's main website.

You can also create a discussion list about a topic and use the wiki to support that discussion. For example, I participate in a videoblogging group that uses Yahoo! Groups for its discussion list. It has a supporting wiki that is used to list videoblogger links and for keeping a running tab of tips and tricks for various aspects of working with video and blogs.

Invitations in Social Networking Tools

While the next chapter is all about community experience in social networks, here we'll talk about both active and passive invitations and participation in social networks in a more general sense.

Passive invitations to participate in social networks come through three avenues: a nice web presence, content, and connecting to someone. Having a nice web presence on a social networking tool can be a challenge because you're usually not given free rein to create something completely unique. For example, you can customize your MySpace profile, but you have to do it within the confines of extra code pasted into text boxes; however, Facebook does not allow customization of its skin, or visual design (though Facebook's skin is attractive to begin with). But, if given an opportunity to experiment with skin designs or colors, work on making yours look different—and making it usable, too. A gaudy skin with unreadable text and unclickable pictures is basically saying "leave me alone" or "don't participate" because no one will be able to do so.

Also, if given the option, make it easy for people to subscribe, join, or comment within the social networking tool. Again, your success might vary with this. Some social networking tools, such as Flickr and YouTube, give you the option of not turning on comments. MySpace gives the option of letting people "friend" you and see your profile only after they have contacted you and you have granted them the ability, which actually has the effect of telling potential participants that you're not really interested in allowing engagement. It will be much harder for people to participate with you. Many will simply choose not to participate.

Now, let's consider content. Content can mean making sure the photos and video displayed on your profile page are done well, are attractive, and have a positive feel to them that draws people in. It can also mean allowing participation via commenting.

Passive invitations in social networking tools also means providing the ability to connect to you in multiple ways, such as allowing friending opportunities and allowing people to find you within the social networking platform by making your feed and your profile public. Providing multiple ways to contact you, via instant messaging, email, and maybe even a phone number viewable by friends, allows further, more private participation to take place.

Active invitations in social networks is also quite varied and will depend on the tool used. The simplest way to actively invite participation is to participate in the network yourself. Don't wait for people to ask to be your friend; instead, find people you want to be friends with and ask to be their friend. In some cases, this also connects them to you and will get your content to them. Friending is what social networking is all about. Without this vital component, social networking really doesn't work.

Another active aspect of social networking is the ability to send direct invitations, as with blogs and wikis. For example, Flickr has Flickr Groups, which can be created around a general topic or be very narrowly focused. For example, the Flickr Groups I belong to include the Henry Doorly Zoo animal photos group, the Librarian Desks group, and a Second Life photo/screenshot group.

Many of these tools also allow you to send event invitations to things such as a speech in Second Life or an art showing through MySpace. You can also send an invitation to watch a video, listen to new music, or read a blog post. The invitation can be sent out via a bulletin board that's sort of like an event listing and invitation.

Organizations that want to improve participation in their digital space might need to learn some new skills. In the last decade or two, writing, producing, and talking were focused on services rendered and brand recognition. The emerging digital landscape allows us to invite participation. Our goal isn't just to convince someone to buy our product or to explain how it works. Now our goal is to jumpstart conversations about our products and services.

Asking via Focus Groups, Surveys, and Analytics

Asking can also be done using traditional web measurement tools. Let's examine focus groups, web surveys, and web analytics to see what types of invitation can be found in each.

Focus Groups

Asking in a more formal setting (i.e., in a physical meeting room, rather than in an online meeting) can take the shape of a focus group. A focus group is "a group of potential consumers used in a market research effort, which is usually designed to determine the likely effectiveness of a product or advertising strategy."[7] The questions are asked in person. Once you have formed the group through asking for volunteers or paying people for their time, ask things such as "What do you like about this redesigned site?" "What do you think of this new service?" or "How do you use our site?" Asking these types of open-ended questions can provide valuable information about your customers and their preferences.

Realize that the responses you receive will be varied and won't usually provide a clear, set direction. You can also get clarification of issues that come up during the discussion time. That's good because the goal of a focus group isn't really consensus or problem solving but to gather enough information about a project for you to have a general feel for the best direction to take. That's invaluable input!

Surveys

While the focus group involves holding discussions with a room full of people, a survey usually doesn't involve warm bodies. Surveys can be found on a website, sent in an email, or handed out on paper. A survey is "the collection of information from a common group through interviews or the application of questionnaires to a representative sample of that group."[8] Both surveys and focus groups are best for asking open-ended questions that allow participants to open up and share their opinions. The difference is that last word: *group*. Focus groups have a tendency to produce groupthink on some topics whereas a survey elicits individual opinions, letting you compare answers to find similarities.

Analytics

Sometimes, you don't even have to ask to find out what people think. How? By using website analytics to guide your design. What types of analytics should you consider for enhancing experience? First, look at the search terms and keywords people use while on your site. Find what terms keep people on a page—what interests them. Find out what's most popular. You can use analytics to show popularity on your main page, and you can use it to show trends on your site, which can help guide future content development. Also, notice what people aren't finding. Discover dead-end pages and the paths people are taking to get to them. This information can show content weaknesses and strengths.

Most importantly, measure the time spent on your site. For example, if you want to measure participation on your blog, a "time on site" measurement is great. If you find that, on average, people are spending one to two minutes a day on specific pages, that most likely means they are reading a blog post. That's wonderful—it's direct evidence of participation. If the content of the blog post just invited the visitor to participate, all the better!

Endnotes

1. "Invitation," Wordnet Search, wordnet.princeton.edu/perl/webwn?s=invitation &sub=Search+WordNet&02=&00=1&07=&05=&01=1&06=&04=&03=&h= (accessed January 29, 2008).

2. "Engagement," Wordnet Search, wordnet.princeton.edu/perl/webwn?s= engagement&sub=Search+WordNet&02=&00=1&07=&05=&01=1&06=&04= &03=&h=00 (accessed January 29, 2008).

3. "Glossary: Participation," Wheel e-Consultation, wheel.e-consultation.org/ wiki/index.php/Glossary_of_Terms (accessed January 29, 2008).

4. Adapted from David Lee King, "Inviting Participation, Part 2: Passive Invitations," David Lee King blog, www.davidleeking.com/2007/01/05/ inviting-participation-part-2-passive-invitations (accessed January 19, 2008).

5. Adapted from David Lee King, "Inviting Participation, Part 3: Active Invitations," David Lee King blog, www.davidleeking.com/2007/01/10/ inviting-participation-part-3-active-invitations (accessed January 19, 2008).

6. "Wiki," Wictionary, the Free Dictionary, en.wiktionary.org/wiki/wiki (accessed October 7, 2007).

7. Michael Motto, "An Advertising Glossary," www.motto.com/glossary.html#F (accessed January 19, 2008).

8. Bureau of Justice Assistance Center for Program Evaluation, "Glossary," www.ojp.usdoj.gov/BJA/evaluation/glossary/glossary_s.htm (accessed January 19, 2008).

Community Building Through Social Networking

What is a social network? It is "a social structure made of nodes (which are generally individuals or organizations) that are tied by one or more specific types of interdependency, such as values, visions, ideas, financial exchange, friends, kinship, dislike, conflict, trade, web links, sexual relations, disease transmission (epidemiology), or airline routes."[1] More simply, social networking is a grouping of people interested in a common goal, hobby, or value.

So, taking that into consideration, what is a digital social networking site?

> A social network service focuses on the building and verifying of online social networks for communities of

people who share interests and activities, or who are interested in exploring the interests and activities of others, and which necessitates the use of software. Most social network services are primarily web based and provide a collection of various ways for users to interact, such as chat, messaging, email, video, voice chat, file sharing, blogging, discussion groups, and so on.[2]

The community-focused experience in many Web 2.0 sites is created through the community-building aspect of these sites—the real-time, or nearly real-time, interaction that can take place among users.

There are many types of social networking sites today, and they can be categorized loosely into two groups: sites about content and sites about people. The content sites focus on a specific type of content, such as photos (Flickr) or videos (YouTube). These sites are extremely social. They allow commenting, RSS feeds, friending, favorites, personal accounts, tagging, and sending private messages to other users.

People sites are similar, but instead of focusing on people's content, these sites focus on the person. The friending, tagging, commenting, blogging, and favorites marking that take place on these sites occur because of interest in the person (or what the person does—hence the popularity of music group sites on MySpace).

Experience and Community

Experience and community occur within social networking sites in a variety of ways, including connections, participation, and a sense of familiarity.

Connections

Connecting with others is the primary goal of most social networking sites. This connection happens directly through *friending*.

When you designate another user as your friend, you create a direct digital connection between that person and yourself. The person is listed in your friends list, and—depending on the social networking site you are using—a variety of other opportunities become available. For example, in Flickr, if you have marked someone as a friend, every time that person adds a new photo to his or her account, you receive a visual notification of that photo. The same thing happens with YouTube and Twitter; whenever your friends update their profiles with new information, you receive a copy of that content. That's one of the primary ways friends keep current with each other via social networking sites.

These connections also lend themselves to conversations via multiple avenues. Some examples are commenting, writing on a friend's wall, sending direct messages or emails, or even vaguely humorous actions like being "poked" in Facebook (a way to send a notification to another Facebook user). Each of these actions has the potential to start a type of conversation, and that conversation leads to community. Facebook and Flickr, for instance, allow you to sign up for topical groups. Then you can participate in focused conversations and share other content related to that topic.

Participation

Obviously, if you are commenting, tagging, poking, and creating and sending content via a social networking site, you are participating in the social networking site's activities. Participation is essential to a social networking site. If no one does anything, there's really no point at all to the site.

Sense of Familiarity

As you view a friend's photos in Flickr, you get to know the person. You see his new car, learn about his house and family, and see the fun things he does. You start becoming visually familiar with that

Flickr friend. In MySpace, you become familiar with a person (or at least an aspect of that person) as you read her thoughts on her blog and through the bulletins she posts. Even subscribing to content feeds via RSS will lead to some type of familiarity because you are reading or viewing something that person has created.

Now that we've discussed social networking sites generally, let's look at some specific sites—Flickr, MySpace, YouTube, Facebook, and Twitter—and see where the digital experience is found in each.

Flickr

As you know, Flickr (www.flickr.com) is a popular social networking site based on people's digital photographs. Flickr works pretty simply: You take a photo, upload it to Flickr, tag it, add a title and description, and ta-da! You're done. Other people can now view, comment on, and tag your images. Each Flickr account, each tag, and each search has an associated RSS feed so that people can subscribe to photos in Flickr in many different ways. For example, I love drumming, so I subscribe to the tag Drumming. This way, whenever *anyone* in Flickr adds an image and tags it Drumming, I receive a copy of that photo.

Flickr offers two primary avenues to a community-focused digital experience, both focusing on communication. The first is visual communication. People communicate visually through Flickr via the photos a person takes. As mentioned earlier, you can get to know people through the photos they take. You see what interests them, and you see their quirks as they take photos of things they find amusing or strange. You are introduced to their families, their pets, and their workplaces. You get to know them visually.

You can also get to know a person through photographic art. You might feel a connection with the work, the technique used, or the person's photographic skill level; in any case, you are connecting with the photographer through the photograph, just as a moving symphony connects people to the music and to the players.

Textual communication is the second form of communication in Flickr. Flickr offers many ways to communicate textually:

- Commenting on photos

- Leaving notes directly on a photo

- Tagging photos

- Sending someone a Flickr email (private message within Flickr)

You can also sign up for a Flickr Group, which lets you communicate with everyone signed up for the group. You are sharing with people who hold a similar interest in something. You can start forum-based conversational threads within the group pages, and you can subscribe to the group's photo pool in a variety of ways.

Besides the conversational benefits, Flickr builds community because of the fun experience of simply getting something for free: You get a copy of everyone's photographs! They send them to you; you don't have to do anything other than mark the people as friends or add the tag's RSS feed to your feed reader. There's something satisfying about a constant feed of something you enjoy that you can view whenever you choose.

MySpace

Flickr is all about photographs; MySpace, on the other hand, is all about people. Started in 2003, MySpace has become one of the most-visited websites in the world. According to Wikipedia, "MySpace is a popular social networking Web site offering an interactive, user-submitted network of friends, personal profiles, blogs, groups, photos, music and videos internationally."[3] MySpace says of itself, "MySpace is an online community that lets you meet your friends' friends."[4]

Community building can be a rich experience in MySpace because it has many Web 2.0 tools and components that help build community. For example, through MySpace, one can add or delete friends; comment on friends' MySpace pages; add content to a blog that goes to the open Web; add content to bulletins that go only to MySpace friends; and add photos, videos, and music (if you set up a music account). If you are using each of these resources to update friends and family about your life, then you are allowing people to know you. If all your MySpace friends are doing the same thing, you are building a relevant community.

The community in MySpace is built on a sense of knowing and meeting people and turning those people into friends and acquaintances. When MySpace is used to share a part of yourself with others, those others get a sense of who you are—what you're doing, who you know, or when you go through a life change. In theory, at least, you can maintain a lifelong connection to your MySpace friends.

That leads us to experience. A new type of continued friendship experience is being created through sites such as MySpace. For example, I didn't keep up with most of my high school friends. I can't tell you what any of them are doing now (I'm a bad friend, I know!). But if I had had a MySpace page (yes, digital networking came along a little after my time), I could have "friended" my friends. I would have been able to keep up with them after high school. I would have known what colleges they attended, what parties they went to, who their boyfriends and girlfriends were, and when they landed that first real job. I would have had an easy and effective way to keep up with them.

Another community-driven MySpace experience is that of meeting people. Some people use MySpace to meet people they otherwise wouldn't meet—very similar to going to a meeting and networking. Finally, there is the experience of control. You control who can be your friend, who can see your profile, and who gets your bulletins. You can even control how your profile page looks. You can add code to your profile page to customize the look and feel and, in some cases, the functionality as well.

YouTube

YouTube says this about itself: "YouTube is the leader in online video, and the premier destination to watch and share original videos worldwide through a Web experience. YouTube allows people to easily upload and share video clips on www.YouTube.com and across the Internet through Web sites, mobile devices, blogs, and email."[5]

YouTube is devoted to user-generated video. Anyone can create a free account (called *channel* in YouTube) to upload video clips. You can tag them, describe them, and share them. Others can watch them, select favorites, and comment. You can embed video or a pointer to the video in an outside blog, web page, or email message to share it outside YouTube.

What types of videos do people upload? Pretty much anything really. Videos range from teenage silliness to short professional presentations and from music videos to commercials to short original shows. Videobloggers use YouTube to share thoughts and to communicate with others.

YouTube allows much community building. Allowing others to watch a video on a topic of interest tends to gather like minds. For instance, the blues harmonica teacher who posts related video to YouTube for his students to view attracts other harmonica players. In this case, the teacher is able to teach others and to create a following, which builds a type of community based on a shared interest in blues harmonica.

Commenting is another way to build community in YouTube. Allowing people to leave comments on videos lets others provide instant feedback after they have watched your video. You can see what they were thinking as they watched it. YouTube even allows for creativity in commenting by providing a way to leave a video comment—which is, as you may have guessed, video that links back to the original.

Listing favorites also builds community in YouTube. If people who marked that harmonica teacher's videos mark all their other favorites, you will most likely have a great resource of harmonica teachers and players, and probably some non-harmonica-related videos as well.

Experience in YouTube is similar to that in Flickr. You are allowed to "be there"—to see and hear an event from someone's point of view. That creates a connection to the video authors. You feel you know them a little bit because you watch them share. YouTube videos tend to be more informal than traditional television or movie videos, so you get to know the video creators. They show an event but also insert their thoughts and feelings and quirkiness into the mix as well.

Then there's the experience of being in control. As with many other user-generated content sites, you can watch YouTube videos at your convenience. It's not a streaming, one-time event that you can watch only at a certain time or place. There's no cost to watch a video, and you can replay it as many times as you like. Users will increasingly expect to have this kind of control over digital content.

Facebook

According to Facebook's website, "Facebook is a social utility that connects people with friends and others who work, study and live around them. People use Facebook to keep up with friends, upload an unlimited number of photos, share links and videos, and learn more about the people they meet."[6] Facebook is different from MySpace in a number of ways. Whereas MySpace has a scattered look, with customized third-party visual templates, Facebook looks clean and uniform—mainly because you really can't customize your profile's visual look. Some recent studies claim that Facebook attracts more people of a higher socioeconomic level than does MySpace, which makes sense because Facebook started as a social networking site for Ivy League college students and opened up only in September 2006 to anyone who wanted to create a profile.

Facebook has all the capabilities of the other social networking sites, including the ability to add friends, comment (via the profile's "wall"), and use private, one-to-one messaging. It also has a "what I'm doing now" option that lets users leave short messages saying what they are doing ("David is … [fill in the blank]"). You can also upload photos and video.

In late 2007, Facebook opened itself up even more, this time allowing non-Facebook programmers to create third-party applications that work with and in Facebook by using what's called the Facebook Platform. "The Facebook Platform is a standards-based web service with methods for accessing and contributing Facebook data."[7] This service allows developers to create applications (apps) that load into Facebook profiles and accounts, and it provides a level of information-sharing and mashing up of Facebook content in new ways. A few examples of Facebook apps include displaying content from other social networking services such as Flickr or Twitter, accessing online documents via apps, and accessing search engines via apps. One of Facebook's goals is to get its users to stay in Facebook even while they are using other social networking tools.

Twitter

As Twitter puts it, "Twitter is a community of friends and strangers from around the world sending updates about moments in their lives. Friends near or far can use Twitter to remain somewhat close while far away. Curious people can make friends. Bloggers can use it as a mini-blogging tool. Developers can use the API to make Twitter tools of their own. Possibilities are endless!"[8]

It's all about me! Not really. But it *is* all about whatever I want to share with people—as long as it's fewer than 140 characters. Some people use Twitter to share little snippets of their lives ("I'm headed to the grocery store!" or "writing about Twitter in a chapter on online community and digital experience. wow.").

Twitter is interesting because it's different. It's sort of like instant messaging but with the added ability to send one message to many people, so it's a one-to-many broadcasting medium. It can be accessed in many different ways, too. I can post via an instant message (IM) client, via the Twitter website, from SMS on my cell phone, from any number of third-party clients and widgets, and even from Facebook via a Facebook application. I can read Twitter Tweets (messages) on all these platforms, too.

Digital experience shows itself in many ways via Twitter. First, there's the community experience. Twitter allows you to feel you've finally "caught up" with friends. With Twitter, you can say things you normally would say on the phone ("Yep, went to the store."). This lets you see a snippet of your friend's life, even the mundane, and you know where your friend is and what he is doing. You feel more involved in the person's day-to-day life. Amazing, since this is all accomplished in up to140 characters.

For me, a favorite experience using Twitter is an "under-the-table" or "aside" conversation. I experienced this for the first time at the 2007 Computers in Libraries conference. We had Wi-Fi access at the conference, so all the geeks in the crowd (sorry—I mean *technology professionals*) were multitasking. We were taking notes, live blogging, tagging Flickr photos, IM-ing, checking work email, and probably listening to the speaker, too.

And we were Twittering. If the speaker said something we disagreed with, we could mention it—sort of like whispering, except you could instantly share your thoughts with everyone following your Twitter feed. And others shared back. So there was an undercurrent of discussion and participation taking place that I'm certain the conference speaker didn't know anything about. It added depth to the presentation that wouldn't have existed at a conference before because, in essence, the attendees were able to talk and discuss during the presentation without having to interrupt the speaker. Of course, we also made dinner plans at the same time. It's all part of the Twitter community-building experience.

What Next?

Now that you know about the community-building aspects of social networking, how can you start incorporating community experience features into your website and your organization? Here are some suggestions.

Pick a Site and Start

Pick a social networking site that sounds interesting or fun to you, and start participating. Explore a few social networking sites first: Does one seem to be a better fit for your organization? Does one have more potential customers? If so, then choose that site as your first experiment. Once you have chosen a social networking site, there are two ways to approach participation:

- Individual use
- Organizational use

You can choose to use the site as an individual. This is simpler because it's much easier to "be yourself" than to "be an organization." Individual use allows you to interact with potential and current customers person to person, which you might not usually experience on a day-to-day basis. This can be valuable because you will get an earful about your services and products! Individual use also allows you to experiment with a social networking site without the added responsibility of getting everything right the first time. If you do something silly as an individual, you haven't damaged your organization's reputation, whereas if you do something silly while officially representing an organization, you might have to do some extra damage control.

Using the site as an organization is slightly more difficult. To be successful, you need to do two things: First, you need to use an authentic, individual voice—you need to come off as an approachable individual, even when representing the organization. Second (and much harder to do), you need to represent the personality or feel of the organization as a whole. Doing both at the same time can be a challenge.

Incorporate Social Networking into Your Website

Once you have chosen one or more social networking sites to use, you can start incorporating content from the social networking site into your organization's website. Many social networking sites allow their content to be embedded into other websites. This is great for organizations because it allows them to share the same content in multiple places. Here are some examples:

- Photos on Flickr can be reused in other websites. The organization can both make its photos highly findable in Flickr through the use of descriptive titles, text, and tags and feature those photos in appropriate pages on its own website.

- YouTube videos can be embedded on other web pages. This allows you to make use of YouTube's bandwidth, storage capacity, and streaming capabilities for web-enabled videos, at the same time making the video available within your organization's own site.

• Twitter conversations can be embedded on other pages. This allows you to display the organization's part of a conversation on other sites.

Successfully using social networking sites can have a positive impact on your customers' experience with your organization. Incorporating your content from social networking sites into your organization's website allows you to share content with more people, reaching a larger potential audience. Actively participating in these sites allows you to interact with your customers. Doing that well provides a positive, memorable experience for your customers and will keep them coming back for more.

Endnotes

1. "Social Network," Wikipedia: The Free Encyclopedia, en.wikipedia.org/wiki/Social_network (accessed October 7, 2007).

2. "Social Network Service," Wikipedia: The Free Encyclopedia, en.wikipedia.org/wiki/Social_networking (accessed October 7, 2007).

3. "MySpace," Wikipedia: The Free Encyclopedia, en.wikipedia.org/wiki/MySpace (accessed October 7, 2007).

4. MySpace, "About Us," www.MySpace.com/index.cfm?fuseaction=misc. aboutus (accessed October 7, 2007).

5. YouTube, "About Us," youtube.com/t/about (accessed August 28, 2007).

6. Facebook, "About," www.facebook.com/about.php (accessed September 4, 2007).

7. Facebook, "Facebook Developers/Support," developers.facebook.com/documentation.php (accessed September 4, 2007).

8. Twitter, "Twitter Support," help.twitter.com/index.php?pg=kb.page&id=26 (accessed September 4, 2007).

PART 3

Customer Focus

CHAPTER 9

What Is Customer Focus?

I've been traveling a lot over the last few years, speaking at library and information industry conferences around the country. I enjoy most everything about the travel—except the hotel beds! My bed at home is the best: My pillow's just right, and when I wake up, I feel rested. Nine times out of 10, a hotel bed is either too hard or too soft, the sheets are scratchy, and the pillows are frequently over-stuffed. When I finally get to lie down for a good night's rest, my head ends up at an odd angle because of the pillows, the sheets bother me, and I just can't seem to get comfortable on the mattress, no matter how many ways I twist and turn.

Then I stayed at a Marriott hotel and experienced the Revive bed. It's awesome! For the first time in a long time, I slept in a hotel bed that felt just right. So, guess what? Whenever I have the choice, I look for a Marriott hotel because I know I'll be able to sleep well when I stay at one.

What did Marriott do to change my hotel experience? It focused on improving the beds—the single most important thing for many frequent business travelers. Actually, Starwood Hotels and Resorts were the first to focus on providing ultracomfortable beds. "The wake-up call for the [hotel] industry may have been the launch of Starwood Hotels & Resorts' signature Westin Heavenly Bed in 1999, which prompted hotel chains to focus on the guest sleep experience. Thus began the 'bed wars,' with major brands swapping out tired bedspreads and mattresses with customized bedding ensembles promising a restful night's sleep."[1]

Marriott has even worked on translating its hotel bed experience to the web:

> Marriott International was thinking along similar lines when it hired T3 Labs to develop an interactive Web site (www.ExperienceMarriott.com) showcasing its "guest room of the future." Using video and cutting-edge Flash technology, the microsite takes visitors through the new room, opening closet doors, turning down beds, turning on showers, and adjusting ergonomic desk chairs. "It's a virtual tour of the bed, the technology, and things users are most interested in," says Amy McPherson, executive vice president, sales and marketing, Marriott International. She adds that Marriott took home the 2005 Gold Adrian award for technology innovation on the site.[2]

Let's look at another example of designing an experience. I have always decidedly *not* enjoyed getting my haircuts at a salon. In fact, around 1992 (after a hairstylist hacked up my hair so badly I had to put up with two weeks of Ross-Perot-hair jokes), I drove to Wal-Mart, bought some hair clippers, and asked my amazingly talented wife if she would start cutting my hair. You see, I had nothing to lose. My experience was so bad that she, with absolutely no haircutting experience, could do a much better job than the last couple of "professionals" I'd been to—and it wouldn't cost me $20.

Even if men are happy with the cut, a lot of us simply don't like the atmosphere of an average salon: the smells, the chitchat, the general feel of the place. Enter Sport Clips. Sport Clips founder Gordon Logan "recognized there was a market niche in targeting just-for-guys hair salons. No longer would a guy have to enter a woman's salon with its smelly perms and hair colors. With over 140,000,000 men nationwide looking for an alternative to typical women salons, Gordon was right on track."[3]

Yes, you guessed it—Sport Clips is a haircutting place for men who like sports. A Sport Clips customer can actually watch sports on big-screen TVs while getting his hair cut. Instead of *Woman's Day* or *Glamour*, the waiting lounge (resembling a locker room in a gym) has sports-themed magazines to read. The interior features sports-themed décor, and there's even sports memorabilia for sale. And the employees are trained specifically to provide a good experience for men: "Our Stylists deliver the ultimate Just-for-Guys haircut experience without the fuss and chit chat of a full service hair salon."[4]

Both Marriott and Sport Clips decided to focus on customer needs and on improving the customer's experience. In both cases, the experience extends beyond the actual product or service. Marriott isn't just providing a comfortable bed. The company's goal is to provide a relaxing guest sleep experience, with the bed as the centerpiece or anchor of that experience. Sport Clips isn't just providing a haircut—every salon does that. Instead, it's providing a male-oriented, sports-themed, TV-watching haircut experience. The actual haircut is just part of the complete experience.

The Marriott and Sport Clips customer experiences were purposefully designed. Now let's look at an example of an experience that is only partly designed by the business. Every year, I go to the excellent Internet Librarian conference in Monterey, California. The conference is held at the Monterey Conference Center, right off Fisherman's Wharf. Right beside the conference center is a wonderful little eatery called Pino's Café. The combination of a great conference and the uniqueness of Pino's Café delivers a delightful, memorable experience.

A group of friends and colleagues usually gathers at Pino's for breakfast and conversation before the conference day begins. We gather there partly because the breakfast food simply rocks (Pino's makes the best omelets I've ever had) and partly because the service matches the food. The waitstaff actually remembers some of us from previous conferences—even our names and what we like to eat. And they have a great sense of humor.

Part of the total Pino's experience does not originate with Pino's itself. The general buzz of a great conference adds to the experience. Catching up with friends and colleagues adds to the mix, too. And then, of course, we're in Monterey. We're by the wharf, so we hear the sea lions barking, and we see the boats and the seagulls … ah, it's delightful! That experience wasn't totally designed, but the combination of friends, great food, authentically friendly staff, and a great location provides a unique ambience and experience nonetheless.

Customer-Focused Experience

The one thing these three experiences have in common is this: All put the customer first. The first two go one step further by purposefully designing an experience for the customer.

So, what is a customer-focused experience? Adam Lawrence, customer experience designer and blogger at workplayexperience. blogspot.com, says this about a customer focus in experience design:

> People are thinking less and less about the product or the service and more about the complete customer experience—the way our customer perceives his contact with us, and the emotions that the experience

invokes. Good experience design can really make your offering stand out from the pack, and command a better price. And with great experience design, you can even turn customers into fans who will keep coming back—and tell their friends.[5]

Nathan Shedroff, a pioneer in experience design, expands the definition as follows:

> Experience Design is an approach to creating successful experiences for people in any medium. This approach includes consideration and design in all 3 spatial dimensions, over time, all 5 common senses, and interactivity, as well as customer value, personal meaning, and emotional context. Experience Design is not merely the design of Web pages or other interactive media or on-screen digital content. Designed experiences can be in any medium, including spatial/environmental installations, print products, hard products, services, broadcast images and sounds, live performances and events, digital and online media, etc.[6]

These definitions have a few things in common. One is a decided customer focus. That makes sense—businesses and organizations don't exist without people! The main reason a business operates is to sell something. Organizations are the same in this respect. They, in essence, are "selling a service," whether or not that selling involves an actual monetary transaction. Take public libraries, for example. A library is "selling" free content, useful information, community memory, and gathering places to customers in the hope that they will interact with both the provided content and with the information professionals on staff. To successfully sell to customers, organizations need a strong focus on delivering a memorable customer experience.

A customer-focused experience attempts to deliver not only customer satisfaction but customer delight. That is what frequently helps a company stand out in a crowd of competitors. For example, Gateway, Dell, Acer, HP, and Toshiba all sell laptop computers. But which laptop-selling company is known for delivering customer delight? Apple. Apple laptop owners are, well, fanatical about the joys of using an Apple laptop. You might remember the previous example of my MacBook Pro purchasing experience and how my Flickr friends commented on a photo of me purchasing the laptop. Would I have received those comments if I had purchased a new PC-based laptop? Probably not. These people (though being tongue-in-cheek) were obviously delighted with their Macs and made sure to share their delight with me.

If customers connect with a product or an organization, it creates what's called customer engagement: "Customer Engagement (CE) refers to the engagement of customers with one another, with a company or a brand. The initiative for engagement can be either consumer- or company-led and the medium of engagement can be on or offline."[7] Also consider this:

> Engagement is a series of customized informational and financial transactions that (1) occur over time and (2) increase both the customer value to the company and the value of the company to the customer. It is not limited to any department, ad campaign, or agency. It needs to be built into everything your company does and everything every employee does. Rather than funneling engagement into brand, creative, and media, engagement should be part of operations, marketing, and overall customer experience. That's how you accomplish profitable and sustainable relationships.[8]

Customer engagement involves creating a bond among the company, the product, and the customer (and even customer-to-customer). Some Mac lovers might fit into this category. There are Mac lovers who already have an iPod, for example, but they will still be in line at their local Apple Store to purchase the newest iPod being released, "just because."

Digital Customer Experience

Now that we have examined customer experience in the physical world, let's look at customer experience in our digital spaces. What does a customer-focused digital experience look like?

Here's one example, from Harley-Davidson. If you visit its website, one of the big directional links you'll see is labeled "Experience."[9] What do you find there? Interestingly, nothing about buying a motorcycle. Instead, you find ride planners, self-guided tour maps, a list of upcoming events, factory tour information, and a link to a "Ride Rewards" program. Nothing about buying motorcycles but everything about enjoying a complete motorcycle experience.

Harley's goal is to make riding a Harley-Davidson motorcycle fun. To make it fun, the company provides activities for Harley owners, making it easy to have fun, with the goal of engaging customers and providing memorable experiences (and selling more motorcycles!).

Kathy Sierra sums it up nicely: "The best user experiences are *enchanting*. … They help the user enter an alternate reality. … In other words, build the thing so that it stays the hell out of the way and lets the user get on with what they really want to do."[10] So one goal in a digital setting, again, is to stay out of the user's way—or, as Steve Krug's book title suggests, *Don't Make Me Think*. The goal is to get customers engaged with "their stuff"—whatever that stuff is. Sierra says, "I don't use a camera to 'use a camera.' I use it to take photos. I want your tool (camera) to stay out of my way so that I can focus on the flow of composing and capturing shots, not working

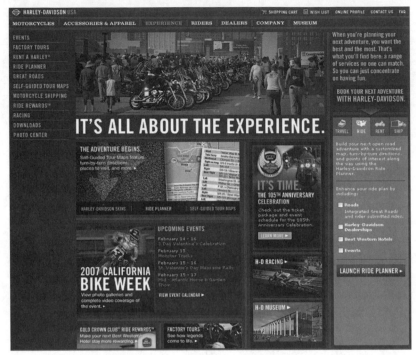

Harley-Davidson's Experience page

out how … to change the shutter speed."[11] She wants to engage with whatever it is she wants to do. The tool is your product, your service, your website, or your web application.

Customers often don't want to interact with you to conduct their business. That's why self-service checkouts and ATMs are so popular. People would rather do the mundane work quickly themselves and save the more specialized services for you, the professional. On a website, you don't want to purposefully get in your customer's way, but you do want to provide easy-to-reach access points for those times when a customer really does need your help. This goes much further than creating simple design and design elements. In some situations, it's a gimmick that works (Sport

Clips). For others, it's simplicity—simplicity in design or in labels to promote easy navigation around the site (Google's main page). To others, such as Pino's, it's just being yourself—being natural and authentic.

In the chapters that follow, let's take an in-depth, customer-focused look at digital experience design and consider some ideas for tweaking your website in order to successfully engage your customers.

Endnotes

1. Erin F. Sternthal, "Industry Watch: Rooms with a View," OMMA, March 2006, publications.mediapost.com/index.cfm?fuseaction=Articles.showArticle&art _aid=40098 (accessed January 22, 2008).

2. Sternthal.

3. Sport Clips, "The Sport Clips Story," www.sportclips.com/AboutSportClips/ TheSportClipsStory.aspx (accessed January 22, 2008).

4. Sport Clips.

5. Adam Lawrence, 12 Show Business Tools for Your Business: A Theatrical Approach to Experience Design, www.experiencedesign.de/twelvetheatrical tools_v1.1.pdf (accessed January 19, 2008).

6. Nathan Shedroff: Experience Design, "Glossary," nathan.com/ed/glossary/ index.html (accessed January 19, 2008).

7. "Customer Engagement," Wikipedia: The Free Encyclopedia, en.wikipedia.org/wiki/Customer_engagement (accessed January 19, 2008).

8. Don Peppers and Martha Rogers, "Customer Engagement Must Actually Involve Customers," www.1to1media.com/View.aspx?DocID=29460 (accessed January 19, 2008).

9. Harley-Davidson, "Harley-Davidson/Experience," www.harley-davidson.com/wcm/Content/Pages/Experience/experience.jsp?locale= en_US (accessed January 19, 2008).

10. Kathy Sierra, "User Enchantment ..." Creating Passionate Users, headrush.typepad.com/creating_passionate_users/2006/03/user_ enchantmen.html (accessed January 19, 2008).

11. Sierra.

Staging and Theming Digital Experiences

In this chapter, we'll look at the Sport Clips experience again (see Chapter 9), but this time we'll observe the planning that went into the experience. Let's review the setup: The waiting area resembles a locker room, the sports memorabilia used for décor is for sale, customers can watch sports on big-screen TVs, and the hairstylists are dressed in sports-themed running suits.

What are Sport Clips' goals? To get men to visit when they need a haircut and to make a profit in the process. But to do that, the company is banking on men feeling more comfortable visiting its place, designed especially for them, than visiting a regular salon.

Think about this for a second. What is it the men who visit Sport Clips are really paying for? Is it a haircut alone? No. There are a lot of haircutting salons, and if I were a betting man, I'd bet there are cheaper places to get a haircut. The service—haircutting—is wrapped up in the experience. That's what visitors to Sport Clips are paying for: the sports theme, or the staged experience.

I first came across the idea of staged experiences when I read *The Experience Economy: Work Is Theatre & Every Business a Stage*. In an earlier article about the experience economy, the authors had this to say about staging experiences:

> Companies will have to learn how to design, sell, and deliver experiences that customers will readily pay for. An experience occurs when a company uses services as the stage—and goods as props—for engaging individuals in a way that creates a memorable event. And while experiences have always been at the heart of the entertainment business, any company stages an experience when it engages customers in a personal, memorable way.[1]

A staged experience is simply one that an organization purposely designs and delivers to customers. The company uses this "stage" to deliver services or goods in hopes of engaging customers by creating a memorable event for the customer.

Now let's translate this to a digital experience. A staged digital experience uses the digital space as the stage, but everything else remains the same. Let's look at some examples to get a better idea of how experiences—and what types of experiences—can be staged digitally.

Home Depot

To begin, let's reconsider Home Depot (www.homedepot.com). The first thing visitors notice about Home Depot's site, as mentioned in Chapter 4, is that it visually resembles the Home Depot stores. Within seconds of visiting the HomeDepot.com site, you see Home Depot's logo, lots of orange (which is the logo color), and lots of large, clear labels, such as Appliances, Building Supplies, and Hardware. This labeling also reflects the physical stores, where large, clear signs all over help shoppers find building supplies. Home Depot's visual look and signage are consistent across its physical and digital spaces.

Build-A-Bear Workshop

How about the Build-A-Bear Workshop? These stores are kid magnets (and I know—I have three kids!). Build-A-Bear Workshops always seem to be filled with kids building bears. They are also filled with other animals, clothes and accessories you can buy for the animals, and the stuffing machines. Build-A-Bear's website (www.buildabear.com) carries the theme from the physical space to the digital space. On visiting its website, you quickly see much of the same stuff you see in the physical store—more bears and more clothes to buy. But you also discover digital-only activities, including online games. The best of these digital-only activities is Build-A-Bearville (buildabearville.com).

What can you do here? When you buy a stuffed animal at Build-A-Bear, the animal's birth certificate includes an Animal ID and PIN number. You use that ID and PIN to register, gain access to Build-A-Bearville, and "bring a furry friend to life online."[2]

Activities in Build-A-Bearville include:

- Decorating a condo for the animal

- Playing games to earn Bear Bills, the virtual currency of Build-A-Bearville

- Customizing your character with "pawsome" fashions and accessories

- Chatting with other kids

Build-A-Bearville

Here's what the company says about Build-A-Bearville on the parent company's information page:

> We want Build-A-Bearville to be a place where your child can grow their friendships with their furry friends as well as their real life friends too. We know that online chat can be a touchy subject so we have worked with parents and industry experts to develop a safe system where you are in control of setting chat options for your child. And the site is monitored for safe socialization. In this new world, your child will be challenged with educational quests and adventures, learn lessons about being responsible citizens of the world and have good real world behaviors reinforced, all in a beary fun new way.[3]

What is Build-A-Bear doing here? The tag line on its site is "where best friends are made,"[4] which is a wordplay on customers *making* bears in the stores. But that tag line also works well for Build-A-Bearville, which is essentially a social networking site. When bear owners sign up for the digital version of their animal friends, they are extending the experience of Build-A-Bear to the online environment.

Webkinz

The Webkinz website (www.webkinz.com) has a great definition of both Webkinz and the virtual world surrounding Webkinz: "Webkinz pets are lovable plush pets that each come with a unique Secret Code. With it, you enter Webkinz World where you care for your virtual pet, answer trivia, earn KinzCash, and play the best kids games on the net!"[5]

The Webkinz site is very similar to the Build-A-Bearville world (although the Webkinz site predates Build-A-Bearville). Upon buying a Webkinz pet, owners can take it home and enter the secret code that comes with each pet. That code grants owners access to Webkinz World. In Webkinz World, they can play games, feed their pet, set up a room for it, buy things for it with virtual money, and chat with other pet owners. Apparently, a pet can even get sick if its owner neglects it: "If your child's pet gets sick (if it has a green snout and an ice pack on its head), please take it to the Clinic in the 'Things to Do' menu. Your child will have to purchase medicine for it to help make it feel better. If a pet is just unhealthy, please feed it some healthier foods and give it some more exercise. Sometimes Webkinz pets get sick if they are left alone for long periods of time without care and their health meter drops below 9 and sometimes they get sick if there's just a sickness going around."[6]

Webkinz World gives Ganz (the company behind Webkinz) the ability to extend its brand into your home. It also allows pet owners

Webkinz World

to extend the fun they have with their pets. Webkinz World allows a pet to come alive in a virtual world and lets the pet owner interact with it there.

Ganz has a savvy commercial model. "When you adopt a Webkinz pet, you get to play in Webkinz World for one year. At the end of the year, you can adopt a new pet onto your Webkinz World account. This will renew your account and all the Webkinz pets on it for one more year."[7] Webkinz is banking on the fact that kids will enjoy the extended experience of playing with and interacting with their virtual pets and other pet owners and that, at the end of a year, kids will buy another pet to continue their pet owner experience in Ganz's digital space.

PBS Kids

PBS Kids also extends its brand, and the viewer's experience, into digital space. For example, take the show *Jakers! The Adventures of Piggly Winks*. (I happen to enjoy this show as much as, if not more than, my kids do.) Viewers can watch the show on most PBS stations and also visit the PBS Kids website devoted to Jakers (pbskids.org/jakers/index.html) to extend the Jakers experience online. There are read-along stories, extra information about each character, coloring sheets to print, and games involving the characters that help to extend the Jakers experience into the online environment.

That's just one show. Most of the PBS Kids lineup has associated digital space where visitors get some form of interaction with the characters (as in games) and a chance to extend the experience for kids—by coloring, playing games, or watching short videos.

Starbucks

I like Starbucks coffee. I don't usually go for the cappuccinos or the lattes—I usually go straight for the grande coffee, no room, and always love it! The stores are fun, too. Customers get the usual coffee and food (for me, often some type of breakfast pastry), but they can also buy things: beverage-related things such as coffee beans, branded coffee mugs, and different varieties of tea, and non-beverage items, such as music CDs.

Guess what? You can extend your coffee aficionado experience on the Starbucks website (www.starbucks.com). Starbucks' site offers quite a lot to visitors. Of course, you can find out about Starbucks coffee. The website says, "Explore every cup—The vast range of Starbucks coffees and our expertise on the subject await. Find out what's being served in stores each week and follow it up with everything you might ever care to know about our roasts."[8]

There is information on every bean sold, with an "order now" button in a handy place on the page. Starbucks also tells you what food to pair each coffee with—and my guess is the suggestion is probably sold at a Starbucks store, too. Under "Coffee Education," you can discover a lot of coffee-related information:

- Coffee taste matcher to help find your "personal taste" of coffee

- Education on tasting coffee: how-to's, what you should notice, and other factors (very similar to wine tasting)

- Information on grinding methods

- Histories of coffee and of Starbucks

- Coffee bean growing regions

Starbucks has purposely extended the Starbucks coffee-drinking experience online through content and sales by packing the website with information on Starbucks, its coffee, and coffee in general. And, they have created easy-to-use shopping areas to buy coffee and coffee paraphernalia online.

Commonalities

We have just considered five very different websites and online experiences. What do Home Depot, Build-A-Bear Workshop, Webkinz, PBS Kids, and Starbucks have in common? They are all working to extend their physical presence into digital spaces, which involves thinking differently about their websites.

Focusing on the Show

In *The Experience Economy*, the authors discuss experience as staging experiences. They also discuss websites as holding pre- or postshows for the "main event," or actual show (held in physical space):

> Our friend Peter Chernack, president of MetaVision Corporation in Burbank, California, advocates using the Web as a "pre-show" (a term borrowed from Disney's use of its queuing areas to set up the "back story" of its rides) to create anticipation for the experience ahead. Shoemaker Vans does this when it streams video from its Skateparks to its Web site so potential customers can view the physical action electronically. ... The World Wide Web can also be used for a dramatic "post-show" experience. We've talked before about how the Experience Music Project (EMP) in Seattle creates mass customized web pages to refer back to the artifacts most enjoyed by its individual guests. Vans documents online every one of its Warped Tour stops, complete with artist list and a gallery of photos.[9]

The sites listed in this chapter have created both pre- and post-shows. Home Depot includes DIY tips on its website, so that before they get to the store, customers know how to proceed with the remodeling project they plan to do, what tools and supplies they'll need, and how hard or easy the job will be to complete. That is an example of a preshow, with the main event being the in-store buying experience. The Starbucks postshow includes detailed information on the coffee you just purchased in the physical store, including where the coffee beans were grown and how to make it yourself (using a Starbucks espresso maker, of course).

Getting Out of the Way

Steve Krug's first law of usability is "don't make me think!"[10] He goes on to say that "all kinds of things on a Web page can make us think unnecessarily."[11] Website visitors really don't want to think about the meaning of some vague text underneath a poorly designed button. Visitors want to think about the "important stuff"—the reason they are visiting the site in the first place. That's why Home Depot's website looks similar to the physical store: to make the experience seamless, familiar, and easy.

Community Connections

Most people don't really want to interact with information or with a website. They want to interact with other real, live people. That's why Build-A-Bearville and Webkinz World are so popular with kids. The kids not only get to play with or meet their stuffed friends in the virtual world, they also get the added benefit of meeting other kids in that same virtual world. They can play games together, visit other kids' pet's rooms, and trade things, just like kids do in physical space. Build-A-Bearville and Webkinz World have both created postshows that extend the toy owners' experience online.

Not About the Product

For most of the sites we've looked at, the point isn't the product itself. It's more about the *feel* of the product, or the experience surrounding it. Webkinz World, for example, doesn't focus on getting kids to buy more Webkinz pets (though you do have to buy another pet after a year of play in the virtual world to continue playing in Webkinz World). The site's goals focus on interaction with the pets—playing games with them, talking to them, and meeting other kids' pets. It's about extending that physical experience into the digital space in a way not really possible in the physical space.

The focus includes extending knowledge of the product. At the Starbucks site, for example, you can find a lot of information about Starbucks' coffees and teas. At Home Depot, you can buy the tools, but you can also learn how to use the tools and materials so that you have the best DIY project possible. And at PBS Kids, you can learn more about each show and the characters in the shows.

These sites all provide great examples of ways to extend an experience to your digital space and to even provide unique digital experiences that can't be mimicked physically. The next chapters focus on providing experiences that delight and engage your visitors.

Endnotes

1. Joseph B. Pine II and James H. Gilmore, "Welcome to the Experience Economy," *Harvard Business Review*, 76: 4 (July/August 1998), balrog.sdsu.edu/~shu/Pine%20WELCOME%20TO%20THE%20 EXPERIENCE%20ECONOMY.htm (accessed January 22, 2008).

2. Build-A-Bear Workshop, "Build-A-Bearville," www.buildabearville.com (accessed December 17, 2007).

3. Build-A-Bear Workshop, Parents' Information, www.buildabearville.com/ parents.aspx (accessed December 17, 2007).

4. Build-A-Bear Workshop, www.buildabear.com (accessed December 17, 2007).

5. Webkinz, www.webkinz.com (accessed December 19, 2007).

6. Webkinz, "For Parents," www.webkinz.com/faq_parents.html (accessed December 17, 2007).

7. Webkinz, "For Parents."

8. Starbucks, "Our Coffee," www.starbucks.com/ourcoffees (accessed December 19, 2007).

9. Joseph Pine II and James H. Gilmore, "Virtual Experiences," experienceeconomy.2yellows.org/wp-content/UserFiles/File/EM0205 VirtualExperiences.pdf (accessed December 26, 2007).

10. Steve Krug, *Don't Make Me Think: A Common Sense Approach to Web Usability*, 2nd ed. (Berkeley, CA: New Riders Publishing, 2006), 11.

11. Krug, 14.

Customer Journey Mapping and Personas

Let me introduce two concepts familiar to marketers but new to many web designers: personas and customer journey mapping. Creating personas and mapping a customer's journey require the experience designer to think through the potential customer experience: how customers might use the organization's website, what the customers' state of mind might be when they arrive at the organization's website, and, most importantly, what drove the customers to the site in the first place.

Customer Journey Mapping

Let me tell you about an airplane experience I had in 2007 (originally published on my blog):

I spoke at New York Public Library a few weeks ago. After my presentation, I decided to show up early at the airport, so I could work on some writing projects (as in a book—stay tuned for more on that one) [yes, it was this book].

At the United Airlines ticket counter, I went to the self-service EASY CHECK-IN counter. One would think that by advertising the counter as EASY CHECK-IN, that it would, in fact, be EASY CHECK-IN. That was not the case.

I received my plane tickets just fine—that part actually WAS easy. But I was there 4 1/2 hours early, and the EASY CHECK-IN machine apparently didn't like that—it wasn't set up to check bags that far ahead. Unfortunately for me, the person behind the counter wasn't much better than the EASY CHECK-IN machine!

I explained my problem (I wanted to check my bags early). Pretty clear, right? Instead of addressing my problem, the Counter Guy simply pointed me to the REALLY LONG LINE for normal ticketing, and said "go stand in that line, and see if they can get you on an earlier flight." WHAT??? That's not what I needed! So I re-explained that I already HAD my tickets (I showed him) and said again "I just need to check in my bag." In a "most patient" tone (you know, that "you must really be a dumb customer but I'm still supposed to be nice to you so I'll talk louder and slower" tone), the Counter Guy restated that I needed to get in the REALLY LONG LINE to see if they could put me on an earlier flight, and that was all he could do for me!

Ok ...

So I headed over to the REALLY LONG LINE. 45 minutes later, when I finally reached the Counter Lady at the end of the REALLY LONG LINE, I explained my problem again (I just want to check my bag). In a very helpful voice, the Counter Lady said "you know, you didn't need to stand in this line for that." (Admittedly, I knew she'd say that, but by this time I realized I wanted to blog about the stupid process I had to go through, so I held out.)

I told her that the Counter Guy at the EASY CHECK-IN counter said I had to stand in this line to get my bag checked in early. So what did the Counter Lady do? She simply rolled her eyes in the general direction of the Counter Guy, and then helped me with my real problem (someone finally took my bag—hooray!).[1]

Now, what was not good about that experience, besides all the obvious things like my long wait, the employee who didn't listen, and the other employee who rolled her eyes? The most important thing I noticed and was thinking about while waiting in that 45-minute line for the wrong thing was this: I wondered if any of the vice presidents at United had ever actually stood in their own line and been treated like an idiot, as I had been. It's just my guess, and I could be wrong, but I suspect that this company had never tested its process on real people and had never checked out all the points of contact, or touch points, that the company has with customers. It hadn't thought through the "journey" I took from entering the airport to boarding the plane.

Let's look at another journey familiar to many of us—the car-buying experience. Does your "car purchasing journey" begin when you walk onto the car lot for the first time? Most likely not. Tom Kelley, popular speaker and general manager of IDEO, doesn't think so, either:

> The journey nearly always has more steps than people first imagine. ... The journey often begins earlier and ends later than people realize. We find it valuable to

consider the emotional underpinnings that precede a journey. The first step in the car-buying journey is not visiting the showroom or scanning the newspaper ads. ... There are usually some preceding steps, catalysts that may be tied to a triggering event (a blown head gasket on your current vehicle). ... Similarly, a car salesman may be tempted to think the journey is over when the customer drives the car off the lot."[2]

According to Kelley, your car-buying experience (and also your experience interacting with the car company) begins before you walk onto the lot and continues after you leave with your purchase. This type of thinking by United about the customer's journey would have given me a much better experience at the airport, don't you agree?

Defining Customer Journey Mapping

With these two examples in mind, let's define two related concepts: *customer journey mapping* and *touch points*. Eric Fraterman of eCustomerServiceWorld defines customer journey mapping as:

a tool for visualizing how customers interact with an organization across multiple channels and touch points at each stage of the customer lifecycle (or part of it). It provides an insight into both functional and emotional needs, a map of the interactions that take place and the emotions created at each touch point. It provides a factual basis to manage change. ... This customer life cycle usually starts when the customer wants or needs to buy a product or service and will continue to the point where the product is reclaimed, redeemed or renewed. The organization's aim is to manage this "journey" in such a manner that maximizes value both for the customer and for the organization.[3]

Another definition comes from the Quality Improvement Agency, a U.K. government agency that supports community college education:

> Customer journey mapping is a process designed to encourage the supplying organisation to think as its customers do about what it is like to interact and do business with them. ... Each point or interaction with your organisation can be referred to as a "moment of truth," a concept first introduced by Jan Carlzon, the former president of Scandinavian Airlines, in his 1986 book entitled *Moments of Truth*. Carlzon defines the moment of truth in business as: "Anytime a customer comes into contact with any aspect of a business, how ever remote, is an opportunity to form an impression."[4]

What can we glean from these two definitions? Customer journey mapping is the concept of mapping out touch points—figuring out when and where a customer will interact with your organization, from the customer's point of view. In the car-buying example, the organization would think through the customer's experience of buying a car, from the moment the customer realizes the need to buy a car to the moment the customer drives it off the lot, and even afterward (extended warranty, continued business). That customer journey has quite a few moments of truth, or touch points, where the organization and the employees "bump into," or interact with, the customer. Journey mapping helps discover each of those touch points, so that the organization can plan what should happen during each interaction. The goal is to make each touch point, or experience, better for the customer—and to, hopefully, make a sale in the process.

What does a digital version of customer journey mapping and touch points look like? Here's what cxpartners, a user-centered design agency, thinks:

> Customer journey mapping is a user centred design technique that brings to life what people are doing on your website or user interface. … Customers don't always take the routes you expect. For instance, most websites are designed around the idea that customers enter at the home page and navigate down into the site. … But thanks to the rise of search engines like Google, most people enter websites somewhere in the middle. And if the site isn't designed well, they'll grab the information they want and head straight back to their search engine. … We apply user testing and user research to map customer journeys. This illustrates areas of your website that users find difficult to access. From there we can improve usability and increase conversions.[5]

Digitally, you need to map out each digital touch point, or each time a customer has the opportunity to interact with the site. Interacting can include many things, such as filling out a form or having to click something, read something, or view something. You can also map out those routes customers take—the entrance points to the major parts of the website and then the pages customers end up on—to make sure customers are finding appropriate areas of the website (and, hopefully, finding what they want).

You can map the experience you want to deliver. What did customers feel like before and after the website visit? Why were they looking for that nugget of information or that product, and did the experience they had while at the site complement their need, somehow resonate with them, or cause a little cognitive dissonance? Good questions to answer for a website!

Here's an example of customer journey mapping using a library's website. As I'm writing this, it's just approaching tax season. Public libraries usually have copies of most tax forms, and the library I work for even offers tax help through a third party. We usually display all this information, plus pointers to tax information, on our website. But do we think through the customer journey, and if so, how would we change our web offerings?

For example, what are customers thinking when they find our tax information? Possibly, they're looking for a tax form. Many libraries create multiple pointers to tax forms of all varieties and even for all states. But does a customer from, say, Topeka, Kansas, really want a small business tax form for Rhode Island? Probably not. Instead of linking to all the tax forms, libraries should point only to the relevant tax information for their primary customers (in this case, customers from Topeka and the surrounding Shawnee County area). Small, brief pointers to more tax information could be included on a secondary page.

The date should also be considered. If it's early January, people have plenty of time to do their taxes. Their tax needs are not yet a pressing need. However, what if it were April 13? They might have a more pressing need then! They wouldn't want to wade through hundreds of out-of-state tax forms. In a perfect world, there would be a big fat link on a page that said, "You're late! Click here to get all the stuff you need to do your taxes now. It's easy, and we'll help you through it!" Or there might be a pointer to an online "taxes for dummies" book that they could browse through quickly. Instead of creating a "traditional" library web page devoted to tax forms, a library could think through the customer's journey and create a much more helpful, dynamic set of information resources. By mapping the customer's journey, you can tailor the content of the site to better fit the customer's needs.

Great—So Mapping Does What, Exactly?

Mapping a customer's journey offers three great advantages for improving the customer's experience:

- Identification of customer interactions
- Insight into customer needs
- Customer focus

Identification of Customer Interactions

Customer journey mapping "'maps' the interactions between your organization and your prospects or customers … from first enquiry through to repeat purchase. … Mapping will analyse timing, frequency, key messages communicated, and media used at each stage of your sales process."[6] Each touch point, or interaction, between the organization and the customer is mapped. This map of touch points provides valuable insight into timing, frequency, and the key messages your customers receive from you and your organization via your website.

Insight into Customer Needs

Journey mapping provides some useful insight into your customers' needs—how they feel during the experience and how your company or organization should treat its customers during each interaction. According to the Quality Improvement Agency, "Customer journey mapping can help the supplier to identify how it 'treats' its customers during each contact that takes place. It should be viewed from the standpoint of how does the customer 'feel' towards the organisation during a particular end-to-end experience. The information gained will help leaders and managers of the organisation to decide what improvements, if any, are required."[7]

Simply changing a single word can improve an experience. For example, the Online Computer Library Center (OCLC) had a website (worldcat.org) that needed improvement. When a user submitted an interlibrary loan request (a way libraries borrow books from each other) on the site, the final page of the process included a grayed-out link back to the search results page and with a large "Goodbye" in the middle of the page. Not very friendly! I blogged about this,[8] and OCLC emailed me to find out more details. OCLC has since changed the "Goodbye" to "Thank you" (a small improvement to the experience) and is working toward a more integrated layout in a future release (a larger improvement to experience).

Customer Focus

Eric Fraterman has this to say about customer focus: "Negative experiences occur typically if the company is at the centre of the universe and the customer is at the end of its processes, with each division or process seeing the customer from its own perspective."[9] Think back to my airport experience again. Who was the center of that set of interactions: me or the airline? Most definitely the airline—I was at the end of the process. Customer journey mapping can turn those interactions around so that customers are at the center of the experience.

Creating a Map

Now that we have a pretty good grasp of customer journey mapping, how do we create one? The simplest way is to start with your staff. You can most likely discover the majority of your customer touch points by having a brainstorming session with your staff: "… capture the major [touch points] … just the key points typically associated with customer interaction. Out of these there will be three or four hot spots that are considered real make-or-break points of an existing or potential relationship."[10]

After you have figured out what your touch points are, you have some work to do. You need to figure out how to improve each touch point to leave the customer with a memorable experience. One idea is to simply ask your customers how to improve those interactions. Ask 10 to 20 of them about the same hot spot, and chances are you'll start to see some similarities in the responses. Then work on implementing your customers' suggestions for each touch point.

Brainstorm with your staff about digital touch points. You can also observe what customers do in any given website task (think usability here). Figure out how they navigate to those touch points, what they do while there, and what they do once they've reached the page of "decision" (the time to buy something or do something). Hold some focus groups and ask what your customers do when they visit your site and what's lacking.

It's especially important to think about the customer's broader journey. What were they thinking before they came to your site? Why do they need your organization's services? How can you tailor your touch points to mesh with the customer's total journey? Answer those questions, and you will have gone a long way toward providing a memorable experience in your digital space.

Personas

Now that we know what customer journey mapping can do for our customers' digital experience, let's try to get even closer to the "individual" by using personas. According to Alison Head, a usability consultant and author of books and articles on usability, personas are "hypothetical archetypes, or 'stand-ins' for actual users that drive the decision-making for interface design projects. ... Personas are not 'made up;' they are discovered as a by-product of the investigative process."[11] As Steve Mulder, of Mulder Media, explains, "A persona is a realistic character sketch representing one segment of a Web site's targeted audience. Each persona is an archetype serving as a surrogate for an entire group of real people."[12]

Kim Goodwin, Vice President of Design and General Manager at Cooper.com, describes the inner workings of a persona in a bit more detail:

> A good persona description is not a list of tasks or duties; it's a narrative that describes the flow of someone's day, as well as their skills, attitudes, environment, and goals. A persona answers critical questions that a job description or task list doesn't, such as: Which pieces of information are required at what points in the day? Do users focus on one thing at a time, carrying it through to completion, or are there a lot of interruptions? Why are they using this product in the first place?[13]

A persona is basically an imaginary person who is a stand in, or representation, of a large segment of your website's target audience. Personas are very helpful in making decisions on interface design and experience.

Developing Personas

The most important thing to keep in mind when developing a persona is that it should be based on real characteristics of real people in that user segment. Mulder says that "to make [personas] credible, you need proof that: Each persona represents real users that you care about. The personas' attributes and descriptions are accurate and complete. The set of personas covers the full range of your users."[14]

Mulder suggests these basic steps when creating personas: First, conduct user interviews, then segment those users on the basis of the information you gathered from the interviews, and finally, create the personas based on those segments.[15] Head suggests starting by gathering demographic data, such as age, education, and job title, of the user segments that will end up with a representative persona.[16] Usability.gov has some further suggestions for ways to gather information for a persona: contextual interviews, individual interviews, surveys, focus groups, and usability testing.[17]

Goodwin goes into more detail about what to gather during a user interview: "In most cases, personas are synthesized from a series of ethnographic interviews with real people, then captured in one to two page descriptions that include behavior patterns, goals, skills, attitudes, and environment, with a few fictional personal details to bring the persona to life. For each product, or sometimes for each set of tools within a product, there is a small set of personas, one of whom is the primary focus for the design."[18]

How Do Personas Help?

Personas can really help web designers create pleasing and useful experiences in their organization's digital space. Instead of trying to create unique experiences for all users, a designer can target three to five personas that represent much larger user populations. According to Mulder, "Personas help you define for whom you're creating the site. Creating personas forces you to spend time thinking about which types of users are critical to your business, so no one wastes precious time thinking about people who don't really matter."[19]

Personas help developers in at least four unique ways:

- Personas bring team members together.
- Solutions are guided by personas.
- Personas build empathy.
- Testing can be done against the persona.

Personas Bring Team Members Together

Personas help bring together team members tasked with creating a website or an application for the site. A persona can help team members "create one shared vision of exactly whom you're designing for and what they want."[20]

When a team shares a common focus—the persona—the customer remains uppermost in everyone's minds, and personal agendas are much less likely to disrupt, or confuse, the planning process. Traditionally, web teams are guided by trends, by watching other websites and mimicking them, and by testing out new parts of the site. All this is great—but not if it takes the team away from focusing on its site's users.

Solutions Are Guided by Persona

Solutions don't have to be guided by the loudest voice on the design team or by the boss' whims. Instead, you can prioritize design solutions based on the personas and refer back to the personas when there's a disagreement over what to do.

Personas even help actively guide the design process. Sometimes, it's hard to decide between the expert user and the lowest common denominator of users who visit the site. Goodwin states: "If you design for the business traveler, the retired bricklayer going to see his grandchildren won't be able to use the system. If you design for the bricklayer, the business traveler will also be happy."[21] And with personas, designers can base these decisions on the bricklayer personas.

Personas Build Empathy

According to Mulder, "Personas help you live in your users' shoes."[22] Using personas helps the design team focus on building the site for the personas instead of designing for the web team's personal likes. If the personas seem real enough (give them a name, such as "Lilly," or even include a picture of the "person" with the description), your team will start designing for that persona. In essence, they'll be designing for an individual. As the Wikipedia definition states, personas "provide a human 'face' so as to focus empathy on the persons represented by the demographics."[23] Some teams, when using personas, actually start asking, "Would Lilly use this?" By focusing on the persona as a person, "the team can avoid the trap of building what users ask for rather than what they will actually use."[24]

Testing Can Be Done Against the Persona

Finally, instead of evaluating the site or the application being built by what the other team members or even other staffers in the office think, designers can evaluate using the personas as a guide. "Team members' solutions can be guided by how well they met the needs of individual user personas. Features can be prioritized based on how well they address the needs of one or more personas."[25]

Testing against personas allows the team to create unbiased evaluations (which does involve a bit of creative thinking since the persona isn't really there). By being creative and getting into the mind of a persona, the team can improve the experience of all the real users represented in the persona.

Endnotes

1. David Lee King, "Bad United Airlines Customer Experience," David Lee King blog, www.davidleeking.com/2007/05/26/bad-united-airlines-customer-experience (accessed January 8, 2008).

2. Tom Kelley, *The Ten Faces of Innovation: IDEO's Strategies for Beating the Devil's Advocate and Driving Creativity Throughout Your Organization*. (New York: Doubleday, 2005), 180–181.

3. Eric Fraterman, "Moving from pipe dream to reality," eCustomerServiceWorld, www.ecustomerserviceworld.com/earticlesstore_articles.asp?type=article&id=2657 (accessed January 6, 2008).

4. Quality Improvement Agency, "The Development Programme for Train to Gain: Customer Journey Mapping," www.qiaemployerled.org.uk/search/Resource-16105.aspx (accessed January 22, 2008).

5. cxpartners, "Customer Journey Mapping," www.cxpartners.co.uk/whatwedo/services/customer-journey-mapping (accessed January 6, 2008).

6. Square Window, "Customer Journey Mapping," www.thesquarewindow.com/services/customerjourney.html (accessed January 22, 2008).

7. Quality Improvement Agency.

8. David Lee King, "Kicking Users Out the Door," David Lee King blog, www.davidleeking.com/2008/01/31/kicking-users-out-the-door (accessed February 15, 2008).

9. Fraterman.

10. Quality Improvement Agency.

11. Alison J. Head, "Personas: Setting the Stage for Building Usable Information Sites," *ONLINE* (July/August 2003), www.infotoday.com/Online/jul03/head.shtml (accessed January 22, 2008).

12. Steve Mulder, *The User Is Always Right: A Practical Guide to Creating and Using Personas for the Web* (Berkeley, CA: New Riders, 2007), 19.

13. Kim Goodwin, "Perfecting Your Personas," Cooper, www.cooper.com/insights/journal_of_design/articles/perfecting_your_personas_1.html (accessed January 22, 2008).

14. Mulder, 19.

15. Mulder, 41.

16. Head.

17. Usability.gov, "Develop Personas," www.usability.gov/analyze/personas.html (accessed January 22, 2008).

18. Goodwin.

19. Mulder, 23.

20. Mulder, 24.

21. Goodwin.

22. Mulder, 23.

23.   "Personas," Wikipedia: The Free Encyclopedia, en.wikipedia.org/wiki/Personas (accessed January 21, 2008).

24.   Usability.gov.

25.   "Personas," Wikipedia.

Customer Focus Ideas

Improving the Ordinary

Have you put antifreeze in your car lately? If so, which kind did you use? Did you buy the 100 percent antifreeze that requires you to find another container to mix in half a gallon of water to get the proper balance, or did you pay the same amount of money for the premixed antifreeze? You actually paid much more if you bought the premixed antifreeze because the containers are the same size and the unmixed is kind of like "concentrate." However, you paid the company for convenience and ease—and for a more pleasant experience. There's no mixing, no holding the container up to the sun to find the liquid line. You simply pour it in.[1]

If you bought the premixed antifreeze, you just bought an experience. Or, you just bought what (for me, at least) was once an ordinary experience, but is now much improved. The antifreeze company greatly improved my antifreeze-adding experience by

adding the water for me, in advance. And, boy, I sure do appreci-
ate it!

On the Web, an ordinary experience can be improved in many
ways, even some that seem normal or invisible to the average user.
Consider, for example, web forms. How can you improve these
forms? I'd suggest reading *Web Form Design: Filling in the Blanks*,
by Luke Wroblewski, who says, "Though knowing most people dislike filling in forms should be reason enough to care about good
form design, there are plenty of other reasons why form design
matters—especially online. On the Web, forms are the linchpins of
ecommerce, social interactions, and most productivity based
applications."[2]

Now let's consider coding. The old way to code and design a
web page was to place most of the design elements within multiple tables. Sometimes these were embedded tables, which ended
up as tables within tables within yet more tables! It was messy
and confusing but made the visual side of the web page look
pretty good.

Unfortunately, this practice of embedded tables also had some
bad side effects. This coding technique sometimes slowed the
loading of individual pages. It also sometimes messed with adaptive technology such as screenreaders, so disabled customers had
a much harder time reading or listening to your site.

Enter cascading style sheets (CSS), a markup language that
enables web developers and designers to separate the code and
the design elements of a page, making design easier. If designers
want to change a design, they simply do it on the style sheet rather
than multiple times on individual pages. CSS also allows designers
to use multiple style sheets, such as a separate style sheet for people using adaptive technology. This provides a better experience
for more users, thus improving what is considered ordinary (and in
this case, it's probably invisible to users).

How about editing digital pictures? Have you ever purchased a
large, professional software package such as Adobe's Photoshop to

do such simple things as crop, resize, and rotate photos to send to Grandma? Many of us have. That's probably considered ordinary by some people. But there are now better ways to do it!

One step better would be to use simpler software, such as Google's Picasa or Apple's iPhoto. Both programs are created for beginners or for people who don't need the powerful editing features that a professional package like Photoshop offers. They're inexpensive, too. Picasa is free, and iPhoto comes free with most Apple computers.

Even simpler would be to use an online editor. There are now some web-based photo-editing applications that feature many of the basic editing capabilities that an average user might need. Pixenate (pixenate.com) is one such app. It allows you to do basic things such as rotating, removing redeye, and cropping photos, all without having to load and purchase expensive software. You just have to have a web browser and go to the website.

An even better example is the recent Flickr/Picnik combo. Flickr, the popular photo sharing and storage site, has teamed up with Picnik (www.picnik.com), an online photo editor, to allow users to do simple things such as auto-fix, rotating photos, cropping and resizing, changing the exposure, changing colors, and removing redeye. The Flickr user simply uploads a photo and then edits it as needed. This has gone a long ways toward improving what was ordinary—editing digital photos—yet difficult for many users.

So, how can you improve the ordinary experiences people have on your website? First, figure out what "ordinary" means for your site. Poke around the major features and touch points of your site. Does your shopping cart do what everyone else's shopping cart does? Is there a way, if you were going to build it from scratch, that you could improve the user experience? Think through these questions, and you're bound to find a way to improve your site.

I'd also suggest comparing your site to sites in other industries. For example, when I redesign, I don't base my designs on other

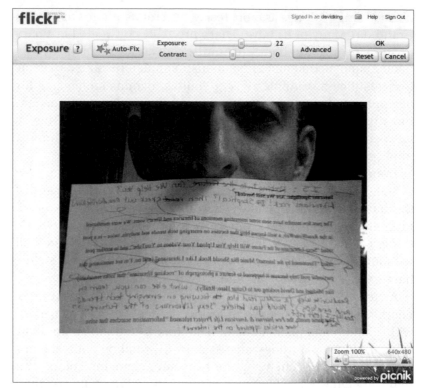

Flickr as powered by Picnik

library websites—if I did, I'd end up with a clone of other library sites that quite possibly copied *my* site at some point! Instead, I look at cutting-edge and popular sites—sites that my customers use, such as Facebook, Amazon.com, and eBay. Then I look at the experience provided on those pages, figure out how to translate those experiences and those functions my library's website, and work from there. This has allowed my web team to move from the ordinary—an average library website—to the extraordinary.

Updating Dinosaurs

A concept related to improving the ordinary is updating dinosaurs. This concept is easy: Think about something that hasn't changed in a very long time, and update it (improving the experience in the process). For example, take paint cans—the nasty, aluminum, house paint variety. Those things haven't changed since before I was born—until recently, that is. Have you been in a paint store lately? Dutch Boy paint cans, for example, are now made out of recyclable plastic (better for the environment); are square instead of round and are made for stacking; have a nice, comfy, built-in handle and no-drip pour spout; and best of all, have a nice big screw-on lid instead of the standard lid that you have to open with a screw driver or special paint can opening tool (which I always tend to lose right before a painting project). Dutch Boy took an industry dinosaur and updated it, improving the experience of many house painters in the process.[3]

Now let me give two web examples of dinosaurs needing updating: lists of links (libraries use these a lot, as do other sites) and newspapers. First, let's discuss lists of links. Traditionally, libraries have created large lists containing thousands of websites, categorized for "easy" finding later on. These huge lists are not easy to use. The concept is a library website dinosaur!

How can we improve? We can turn the lists into something called a subject guide. Ever visited About.com, with its subject-specific guides? Some libraries have started mimicking that subject guide model, combining the subject-specific list of web links with all the library's other cool content for a certain subject area. Say, for example, the library has content on travel. Usually, this travel content would be separated throughout a website: The travel books would be found in the catalog, the articles in magazines would be found in the databases section, the links in the list of links page, and any related programs in the calendar of events. Why not mashup all that stuff into one big, happy travel guide? Or even go one further, and add a blog, too? That way, when something new gets added to the travel subject guide (for example, a new travel-related web link), you have the ability to post about it and alert users to the update.

Also, the library could transfer its list of links over to a Delicious (a web-based bookmarking service) account, which is cool because all librarians can easily get to it and add to it. It's searchable, browsable, and taggable—more so than any in-house list I've seen. Plus, it's social: It allows users to subscribe to the list, which alerts them that their library thinks this link is important.

Now let's consider newspapers. The dinosaur online newspaper is strictly a destination site: Customers *must* go to the site to read the articles. The newspaper might send its customers email alerts, but instead of sending them an article, the alert points customers back to the newspaper's website. The website then assails them with annoying pop-up ads and offers neither (RSS) feeds nor anyplace to make comments; instead, customers are directed to send an email to the "Letters to the Editor" section. And the news? It comes only from the official reporters.

But what are CNN, the BBC, and *USA Today* doing? They have updated the newspaper model quite a bit. Each offers many news delivery options: letting you read articles on the site and use email alerts, RSS, and even Twitter feeds for updates. Multimedia is rampant—lots of video and podcasting, which changes the normal print newspaper (in *USA Today*'s case) into an interesting emerging model of mixed media instead of a traditional model tacked onto a website. And letters to the editor? Who needs them now that these three sites have given all readers the ability to leave their thoughts with the articles (unheard of in a traditional newspaper model)? In some cases, the commenters turn into reporters, blurring the line between traditional media and citizen journalism. This definitely updates those dinosaurs!

Merit Badging

Now, let's look at an interesting concept called merit badging. According to Tom Kelley, author of *The Ten Faces of Innovation*: "The trend watchers at Iconoculture say there's an emerging lifestyle pattern called 'merit badging.' The idea is that large groups of people, having climbed psychologist Abraham Maslow's hierarchy to the point where they feel they have amassed enough stuff, are now collecting experiences."[4] Collecting experiences? How cool is that? Here are some examples: Some people collect countries—figuratively, by visiting them. Or, they may collect book series—as in reading all the *Hardy Boys* books.[5] "Visitors to Japan may have noticed that virtually every major train station, tourist attraction, and hot spring spa provides an oversized rubber stamp for making an imprint on your travel journal or notebook. ... Incredibly, the whole country has turned traveling into a game."[6]

Merit badging has even affected my family to a certain degree. For example, the Christmas when my oldest daughter was 12, she received the usual haul of presents, but she also received cake decorating and horse riding lessons—both squarely in the merit badging experience realm. Two collected experiences!

Organizations have to think in terms of rewards to turn merit badging into a business model. As Kelley suggests: "Pick out your best, most loyal customers, and help them become connoisseurs of your product and service. If they have sampled half your offering, tempt them with the other half. Give them a reward, a symbol, a stamp on their passport, a gold star. Your best customers are hungry for new experiences. Help them fill their stash."[7]

Examples of collecting experiences and merit badging already exist online. I offer these examples to give you some insight into this emerging trend and jumpstart your thinking about things you can do to get your customers or visitors interested in merit badging on your site.

Flickr allows people to collect experiences and offers a couple of unique merit badging experiences. The first experience is more of a collection helper: the Flickr account itself. Each Flickr user has the ability to create sets and groups of photos about a trip, a thing (like techie toys), a pet, or some other interest. It's fun to put photos into sets, so that your pictures are arranged nicely and neatly, and into groups, so that you can share your images with others who share similar interests. Both tools are great ways to organize collections of pictures online, but they are even more powerful as a memory organizer.

Flickr allows anyone to set up a free account. If you want to go to the next step, you can pay next to nothing to turn your account into a "pro" account. When you go pro, you get a little "pro" badge by your name. This is a great merit badge technique because you not only get a few more bells and whistles (extra storage space is one biggie); you also get an actual badge by your name that tells the world you are, in fact, a pro user of Flickr.

Friending is another type of merit badge because you can collect friends. If you see other photographers' photos you like, you can "friend" those photographers. Hopefully they'll want to friend you, too, and *voilá!* Suddenly you're collecting friends.

RuneScape, a free online game set in a medieval fantasy world filled with knights, wizards, goblins, and dragons and played by around 400,000 people at any given time, has a couple of interesting merit badging techniques, so it's a very social game. In RuneScape, you can walk around randomly doing things, or you can participate in *quests* (challenges). Quests usually require some combination of puzzle solving, killing things like vampires, and collecting things for nonplayers (taking an old sword to the king, for example). When you complete the quest, you get prizes—fancy swords and money. Upon completion, the quest gets marked off as "done"—a merit badge in your account. Merit badging comes into play here because you suddenly feel compelled to complete each quest!

Another type of merit badging in RuneScape is the free versus fee parts of the world. When you start out in RuneScape, you get placed in the free part of the world. You can participate in quests, interact with other players, kill goblins, earn in-world money, and more. But there's a gate you can't cross that goes into the fee part of the world. It's much larger than the free part and has some interesting things to do, such as fighting higher-level monsters and gaining access to additional quests.

Merit Badging on Your Site

What types of merit badging can you incorporate into your website to make users want to come back again and again? Here are some ideas:

- Give them something as an incentive. Can you create a coupon for customers buying certain items or participating in upcoming events? The coupon will tempt customers to come back for more.

- As with the Flickr example, designate users at a certain level as "pros" and provide them with a visible badge of some type. Decide what comes with a pro membership—in Flickr's case, it's more space to store content and more bandwidth to upload photos.

- Reward your busiest and best customers. Two extremely busy websites are eBay and Amazon.com. What do they do? eBay gives a visible badge to top sellers. It's a mark that any seller would want on eBay because it indicates integrity, consistency in selling, good quality, and so on. Amazon.com does something similar with the top reviewer tags it provides to popular book reviewers. These people get noticed via a visual badge signifying who they are.

One last thought. Why not connect the merit badging technique to the website before or after a physical event? Think of it as a pre- or a postshow for your site. For example, customers get a haircut, visit the hair salon's website afterward, enter a confirmation number they received at the salon, and receive a discount for their next haircut. This is a way of connecting the customer back to the organization's digital space. You will garner extra visits by providing incentives to keep customers coming back. It's a type of merit badge in the guise of a coupon.

Endnotes

1. Tom Kelley, *The Ten Faces of Innovation: IDEO's Strategies for Beating the Devil's Advocate and Driving Creativity Throughout Your Organization* (New York: Doubleday, 2005), 170.

2. Luke Wroblewski, *Web Form Design: Filling in the Blanks* (Rosefeld Media, 2008), 5.

3. Kelley, 176.

4. Kelley, 189.

5. Kelley, 190.

6. Kelley, 191.

7. Kelley, 192.

CHAPTER
13

The Next Step

I can't wait to see what these ideas, joined with your creativity, will produce (in fact, feel free to share your cool creations with me at davidleeking.com/digitalexperience). Before sending you off with some last thoughts, let me offer a quick review.

We have looked at several key ideas:

- **Structure** – In order to offer a digital experience, you first need a digital space. We discussed building that space and what to think about during the building phase.

- **Community** – Once you build the space and invite people, they will (you hope) participate—with you, with your products and services, and maybe even with each other. We looked at pointers for providing a great experience through digital community.

- **Customers** – Who do you want to visit your site? Your customers! We discussed ways to stage experiences for your customers.

For each of these elements, the ultimate goal is to connect with the customer or website visitor in a few different ways:

- **Connect the customer to the company** – Remember those Apple evangelists I spoke about in Chapter 1? They are connected to their favorite company. As I write this, it's about 12 hours before Steve Jobs gives his annual MacWorld keynote speech. When he does, thousands of Mac users will hang on his every word and then dissect each word shortly thereafter. Those people are definitely connected to Apple, the company.

- **Connect the customer to the product** – What do I do multiple times every hour? Visit Google. No, not to do inane searches on random topics. I visit Google to check my email and read RSS feeds. I have definitely connected to Google's products (I'm even wearing my way cool black Google T-shirt that came with a server. Oh, my ...).

- **Connect the customer to the extras** – Today on Facebook, for instance, I checked my Flickr feed, read a funwall post, Twittered, and fought some vampires. All of these are Facebook applications created by third parties, not actually by Facebook itself. Facebook provides the digital space and allows other groups to provide the fun I just had. Hence, the extras.

- **Connect the customer to other customers** – This can happen in many ways, including blogs, photos, videos, microblogs such as Twitter, or even a discussion forum. These sites provide a way for people to connect to others.

The main goal of experience design isn't to simply provide a fun experience for customers. It is to figure out a way to connect your customers with something that will create a positive, lasting impression. Doing so will lead to loyal business for you, a better experience for your customer, and the potential for customers to help others in ways previously unattainable. Amazon.com's customer reviews are a great example of this.

So where do we go from here? Here are just a few ideas.

Work on Those Websites

Think about your recent web journeys lately. Have you visited a site that was hard to use? That didn't give you the information you needed? That gave you the information but left you feeling frustrated? That gave you, in other words, a negative experience? I'm sure you did. Now think about your website. How do visitors feel when they leave it? And how do you know? These are some great questions to ask your customers or website visitors.

If you already have an amazing website, improve it anyway! Lead us feeble web followers who need to see your next cutting-edge example of experience design at its finest.

Create Some Experience Stages

Adam Lawrence suggests a great way to think of staging: "Your customer touchpoints—your retail location, your hotel, your Web site, your brochure—are your 'stage sets.' Arrange them to mirror the Boom-wowowow-BOOM! of your storyboard as people move through the experience (or as it unfolds around them)."[1] So, your goal as "director" of your digital space is to get the members of your team dancing—train them to dance on your stage. Lawrence explains, "Whether you are a doctor or a plumber [or web designer, or writer, or the comment answering guy, or the videographer], every part of your customer contact is like performing a show—after all, you are trying to manage the perception that the customer forms of you and your offering. So *rehearse*! Rehearsal is a great time to play around with new ideas (promoting creativity and motivating your team), as well as getting those standard situations down pat."[2]

What do actors and musicians do besides memorize lines or music and perform? They connect. They connect with the audience. That's really their job. And that's your job, too—to connect with your customers. Think about it. Let's say you have the option to buy one of two shirts: one shirt from some impersonal big box retailer, and another shirt, for the same price, at a store where the clerk is interested in you, suggests a belt to match, and gives you a coupon for your next visit. Which place are you going to shop? Which place will you visit again? You know the answer. That's because the clerk connected with you, the customer, not by being pushy or fake but by being genuinely nice and by working to connect with you in some way.

Connecting with customers needs to happen on the web, too. To do this, you need to learn to interact on the web. Training (should there be any) needs to include how to connect and how to interact with others while using the tools of writing or photographing or making video. The experience your visitors have while on your site, and while attempting to interact with you, your products, and your content is the experience.

Work on Conversation

We need to work on our conversations to improve our ability to connect and interact. Michael Kaufman points out: "Call it the conversation economy. One of the engines driving online growth is the fact that communities are forming around popular social platforms such as YouTube, Facebook, Flickr, Ning, Twitter and the rest. These platforms facilitate conversation, and markets are now conversations, as *The Cluetrain Manifesto* pointed out years ago. Conversation leads to relationships, which lead to affinity."[3] Conversations have become the way to market, so we need to learn the fine art of conversation in many different formats—for instance, writing and sharing photos and videos. It's the same old skill—conversation—presented in a new, digital-age wrapper.

Work on Organizational Change

Finally, we need to work on our organizations. This book presents ideas that are different from the traditional ways of building websites. Rather than thinking so much about the structure and content of the site, we need to think about the experience that the structure and content can provide. Yes, folks, change is in the air. And we all know that change is hard!

Successful transitions are needed for organizational change to happen. The transition to an experience economy and to markets as conversation is already happening for your customers, hence the popularity of sites such as eBay, Amazon.com, craigslist, and Facebook. The rest of us need to catch up!

When you build a great looking, user-friendly website that aims to connect with and engage your customers, you're well on your way to successful digital experience design. So dream big. Work hard—so your customers don't have to. Be transparent. Work in "beta mode." It's your chance to create a better world—online and off.

Endnotes

1. Adam Lawrence, "12 Show Business Tools for Your Business: A Theatrical Approach to Experience Design," www.experiencedesign.de/twelve theatricaltools_v1.1.pdf (accessed January 15, 2008).

2. Lawrence.

3. Michael Kaufman, "The Experience Economy Is Becoming the Conversation Economy," Innovation Labs LLC: Field Notes on Innovation and High Performance, www.innovationlabs.com/blog/2007/04/experience-economy-is-becoming.html (accessed January 22, 2008).

RESOURCES AND RECOMMENDED READING

Part 1: Structural Focus

Books

37signals. *Getting Real: The Smarter, Faster, Easier Way to Build a Successful Web Application.* Chicago: 37signals, 2006.

Garrett, Jesse James. *The Elements of User Experience: User-Centered Design for the Web.* San Francisco: New Riders Press, 2002.

Krug, Steve. *Don't Make Me Think: A Common Sense Approach to Web Usability.* 2nd ed. Indianapolis, IN: New Riders Press, 2005.

Morville, Peter. *Ambient Findability: What We Find Changes Who We Become.* Portland, OR: O'Reilly Media, 2005.

Nielsen, Jakob, and Hoa Loranger. *Prioritizing Web Usability.* Indianapolis, IN: New Riders Press, 2006.

Rosenfeld, Louis, and Peter Morville. *Information Architecture for the World Wide Web: Designing Large-Scale Web Sites.* 3rd ed. Portland, OR: O'Reilly Media, 2006.

Zeldman, Jeffrey. *Designing with Web Standards.* 2nd ed. Berkeley, CA: Peachpit Press, 2006.

Websites

Adaptive Path Blog, www.adaptivepath.com/blog
Creating Passionate Users (Kathy Sierra), headrush.typepad.com
David Lee King, www.davidleeking.com
Logic + Emotion (David Armano),
      darmano.typepad.com/logic_emotion
Signal vs. Noise (37signals), www.37signals.com/svn

Part 2: Community Focus

Books

Barabasi, Albert-Laszlo. *Linked: How Everything Is Connected to Everything Else and What It Means.* New York: Plume, 2003.
McConnell, Ben, and Jackie Huba. *Citizen Marketers: When People Are the Message.* Chicago: Kaplan Business, 2006.
Rheingold, Howard. *Smart Mobs: The Next Social Revolution.* Cambridge, MA: Basic Books, 2003.
Scoble, Robert, and Shel Israel. *Naked Conversations: How Blogs Are Changing the Way Businesses Talk with Customers.* New York: John Wiley & Sons, 2006.
Surowiecki, James. *The Wisdom of Crowds.* New York: Anchor, 2005.
Tapscott, Don, and Anthony D. Williams. *Wikinomics: How Mass Collaboration Changes Everything.* New York: Portfolio Hardcover, 2006.

Websites

Facebook, www.facebook.com
Flickr, www.flickr.com
MySpace, www.myspace.com

ReadWriteWeb, www.readwriteweb.com
Rocketboom, www.rocketboom.com/vlog
Second Life, www.secondlife.com
Tame the Web (Michael Stephens), www.tametheweb.com
Twitter, www.twitter.com
YouTube, www.youtube.com
Ze Frank, www.zefrank.com

Part 3: Customer Focus

Books

Kelley, Tom. *The Ten Faces of Innovation: IDEO's Strategies for Beating the Devil's Advocate & Driving Creativity Throughout Your Organization.* New York: Doubleday, 2005.

Klingmann, Anna. *Brandscapes: Architecture in the Experience Economy.* Cambridge, MA: MIT Press, 2007.

Krug, Steve. *Don't Make Me Think: A Common Sense Approach to Web Usability.* 2nd ed. Berkeley, CA: New Riders Publishing, 2006.

Lasalle, Diana, and Terry A. Britton. *Priceless: Turning Ordinary Products into Extraordinary Experiences.* Cambridge, MA: Harvard Business School Press, 2002.

Pine, B. Joseph II, and James H. Gilmore. *The Experience Economy: Work Is Theatre & Every Business a Stage.* Cambridge, MA: Harvard Business School Press, 1999.

Pine, B. Joseph II, and James H. Gilmore. *Authenticity: What Consumers Really Want.* Cambridge, MA: Harvard Business School Press, 2007.

Smith, Shaun, and Joe Wheeler. *Managing the Customer Experience: Turning Customers into Advocates.* London: FT Prentice Hall, 2002.

Websites

Church of the Customer Blog (Ben Mcconnell and Jackie Huba),
     www.churchofthecustomer.com/blog
Curious Shopper (Sara Cantor), curiousshopper.blogspot.com
Customer eXperience Crossroads (Susan Abbott), www.customer
     crossroads.com/customercrossroads
Customer Service Tips & Perspectives (Eric Fraterman),
     customerfocusconsult.blogspot.com
Experience Evangelist Blog (Jeff Kallay), blogs.targetx.com/
     targetx/theexperienceevangelist
Experience Manifesto (David Polinchock), blog.brandexperience
     lab.org/experience_manifesto
Experience Matters, experiencematters.criticalmass.com
Experience Solutions (Damian Rees and Ali Carmichael),
     www.experiencesolutions.co.uk/blog
Experienceology (Stephanie Weaver),
     experienceology.blogspot.com
Good Experience (Mark Hurst), www.goodexperience.com/blog
Logic + Emotion (David Armano),
     darmano.typepad.com/logic_emotion
NextUp (Doug Meacham), nextup.wordpress.com
Picknik, www.picnik.com
Pixenate, www.pixenate.com
PoetPainter: Designing for Experiences (Stephen P. Anderson),
     www.poetpainter.com/thoughts
Putting People First (Mark Vanderbeeken),
     www.experientia.com/blog
Re-Imagineering, imagineerebirth.blogspot.com
Total Experience, totalexperience.corante.com
UX Magazine, www.uxmag.com
Work•Play•Experience (Adam Lawrence),
     workplayexperience.blogspot.com

GLOSSARY

API. Application Programming Interface. A set of functions that allow one application to communicate with another application.

Atom feed. A syndication format using the XML markup language for web feeds; similar to RSS feeds.

Behavior mapping. An observation technique used to record, or "map out," the activities of people occupying a space. Observations are recorded on a plan of the space, and a "behavior map" is created.

Beta. A pre-release stage of software and web applications. Many Web 2.0 companies release beta products in order to watch real users interact with their product or service, then use these interactions to continually improve the product.

Blog. Shortened form of "weblog," a website featuring regular entries displayed in reverse chronological order, so the newest posts, or articles, appear at the top of the list. Blogging software makes it easy for authors to post, add categories and titles, and receive comments on each post.

Cascading style sheets (CSS). Language used to define the style and formatting of things like fonts, font size, color, or spacing in an HTML document.

Commenting. A way of allowing others to add their thoughts to online content.

Content management system (CMS). A software application that manages and organizes websites, which makes web publishing easier for nontechnical users.

Contextual navigation. Navigational elements included in the main content of a web page. Links appearing in text and hyperlinked images are examples of contextual navigation.

Customer journey mapping. Tracking and describing the set of experiences a customer encounters when interacting with a service or making a purchase.

Delicious. Social bookmarking service that allows users to store bookmarks online and access them using any computer with access to the web.

Destination site. A website or portal where visitors can interact with others or with content. RuneScape (an online game) and YouTube (a video sharing website) are two examples of destination sites.

Digital rights management (DRM). Technology that protects the digital rights of content like music, video, or text.

Experience. Interaction with some thing or some event, through situations, emotions, or sensations.

Experience economy. Described by Pine and Gilmore in a book by the same name, first published in 1999. In an Experience Economy, one sells an experience, using goods and services as props for the "event."

Facebook. A social networking website that connects people. Facebook started in the academic community, but now offers accounts to anyone with a valid email address.

Facebook platform. A coding language and set of APIs that allow developers to build Facebook applications.

Feed reader. A web- or desktop-based application that aggregates syndicated web content for easy access.

Flickr. A web-based photo management and sharing application.

Focus group. A group of people gathered for the purpose of obtaining perceptions or opinions, suggesting ideas, or recommending actions about something presented to them.

Folksonomy. Also known as tagging, a personal labeling system for items found on the web.

Friend/Friending. The act of marking someone as a contact in a social networking service.

Global navigation. Website navigation that appears on every page of a website.

Information architecture (IA). A way to build the structure of a website using navigation, labeling, and search.

Instant messaging (IM). Software that allows two people to communicate in real-time using a text-based chat system.

Invitations (passive and active). The act of inviting people to participate in activities on your website. Active invitations could include directly asking for participation (e.g., in the form of a written question), while passive invitations could include writing great content and designing a user-friendly comment form.

JavaScript. A scripting language used on websites.

Local navigation. Navigation on a single page of a website.

Markup language. Coding language surrounding text that describes how that text should be structured and formatted.

Mashup. The combination of content from multiple services into a unique, derivative work.

Mediawiki. The company that created the wiki software that powers Wikipedia.

Merit badging. An emerging lifestyle pattern of collecting experiences rather than things (e.g., visiting all 50 states of the United States of America).

Microblogging. A form of blogging created with short posts of 200 words or less.

MySpace. A social networking service that connects people. MySpace allows a great deal of customization on members' accounts.

PERL script. An open source programming language created in 1987 by Larry Wall. PERL was originally developed for text manipulation and is still used for a variety of web development projects.

Personas. Created characters that represent different user types within a targeted demographic.

Ping. A basic Internet program that verifies if specific IP addresses exist and are reachable online.

Poking. An activity in Facebook that sends another user the message that someone "poked" you. Then you can reciprocate if desired.

Really simple syndication (RSS). A way for website users to subscribe to parts of a website.

RSS feed reader. *See* Feed reader.

RSS newsreader. *See* Feed reader.

RSS reader. *See* Feed reader.

RuneScape. A massively multiplayer online role-playing game (MMORPG) created by Jagex. It has a fantasy/medieval theme.

Scenarios. A description of several hypothetical situations.

Scope. A description of project boundaries.

Shadowing. Watching a customer interact with a product, service, or location and noting observations.

Short message service (SMS). Also known as Text Messaging. Short messages sent to a mobile device.

Skeleton. The wireframe or minimal form of a website.

Skin. A graphical theme or appearance that can be added to web services and tools to personalize the tool for the user.

Skin customization. The process of editing a skin or theme.

Social network. A social structure tied to individuals using a common web-based tool or service.

Specifications. List of components, requirements, and deliverables for a web project.

Stickiness. Ability of a website to hold visitors' attention.

Strategy. Plan of action designed to meet organizational goals.

Structure. The act of building a website.

Surface. The visual look-and-feel of a website.

Tagging. *See* Folksonomy.

Text messaging. *See* Short message service (SMS).

Third space. A concept that focuses on a third social surrounding, separate from most people's first two social surroundings of home and work.

Touch point. Each customer interaction or encounter with your organization that can influence the customer's perception of your product, service, or brand.

Trackbacks. A method for web authors to request notification when somebody links to one of their documents.

Twitter. A microblogging tool that allows users to send quick messages of 140 characters or less to Twitter friends.

Usability. The process of making your site easy for customers to use.

Usability testing. Testing how easy your site is for customers to use.

Videoblog. A blog that posts video-based content.

Videocasting. *See* Videoblog.

Wall. A place to leave comments for users of Facebook.

Way finder. Also known as signage.

Web 2.0. A new set of web-based tools, services, and philosophies that focus on open access to content, APIs, conversation, sharing, and community.

Website analytics. Measurement and analysis of a website through statistics kept of website usage.

Wiki. Website application that allows visitors to add, remove, and edit website content.

Wireframe. A visual tool for presenting functionality and structure of a website.

XML. eXtensible Markup Language. Allows developers to define data formats.

YouTube. A web-based video hosting service and social network.

ABOUT THE AUTHOR

David Lee King is the Digital Branch and Services Manager at the Topeka & Shawnee County (Kansas) Public Library, where he plans, implements, and experiments with emerging technology trends. He has spoken at information industry events in the U.S. and internationally about emerging tech trends, website usability and management, digital experience design and planning, and managing tech staff. He has been published in numerous library industry journals and, with Michael Porter, writes the "Internet Spotlight" column in *Public Libraries Magazine*.

Kansas governor Kathleen Sebelius recently chose David to serve on the board of directors for the Information Network of Kansas, and *Library Journal* named him a "Mover & Shaker" for 2008. David writes a popular blog that focuses on emerging tech trends, tips, and tools at www.davidleeking.com.

Before discovering his niche in the information industry, David held many jobs, including pizza delivery dude, customer service representative at a mutual fund company, housepainter, disc jockey, and freelance recording engineer. When not working, writing, or speaking, David enjoys writing songs and creating videos (posted at www.davidleeking.com/etc), as well as spending time with his amazing wife and his three cool kids.

INDEX